The 10 TEN
Commandments

The 10 T E N Commandments

Timeless Challenges for Today

MITCH FINLEY

Liguori

LIGUORI, MISSOURI

*This book is for Charles McNeill,
a friend all down the line.*

Published by Liguori Publications
Liguori, Missouri
http://www.liguori.org

Library of Congress Cataloging-in-Publication Data

Finley, Mitch.
    The Ten commandments : timeless challenges for today / Mitch Finley.
       p. cm.
    Includes bibliographical references.
    ISBN 0-7648-0663-7 (pbk.)
      1. Ten Commandments—Criticism, interpretation, etc. 2. Christian ethics—
Catholic authors. 3. Catholic Church—Doctrines. I. Title.

BV4655 .F466 2000
241.5'2—dc21   00–042354

Printed in the United States of America
04 03 02 01 00   5 4 3 2 1
First Edition

CONTENTS

INTRODUCTION

S omething there is in the modern heart—including the modern Catholic heart—that reacts negatively to the word *commandment*. "Whoa! Wait a minute. Who's commanding whom around here, anyway? Let's 'dialogue' about this before anybody goes around commanding anything, okay?"

The word *commandment* conjures up images of somebody giving orders. "You'll do as you're told, and you'll like it, see?" Modern folks don't appreciate the idea that anyone is going to *order* them to do *anything*. We cherish our personal liberty too much for that. "*I* will decide what I'm going to do, and how and when. Nobody is going to tell *me* what to do!"

"Commandment" smacks of *authoritarianism*. It's *undemocratic*. Authoritarians are people who throw their weight around; people who lord it over others—generals, admirals, bosses, CEOs, prison guards; people who yell "Jump!" and expect other people to ask "How high?" We don't like this whole scenario one little bit.

Given this mind-set, when we hear that God, the Creator of the Universe, the Big Guy Upstairs (pardon the bad theology of this last image of God), has some "commandments" for us, we are naturally suspicious. "We thought you said that 'God is love.' How could a God who is love lower the boom in the form of *commandments*, and *ten* of them, no less? Don't we even get to take a *vote* on this?"

WORDS OF WISDOM

The Ten Commandments come from the Bible, of course, and the various biblical documents originated in cultures and societies far, far away, and a long, long time ago. Therefore, the possibility for misunderstanding is more than slight. It's to our advantage to ask a few questions and do some research before we call in the cavalry to rescue us from a wild-eyed God with commandments on his mind.

First let's address our problem with the word *commandment*. Sometimes instead of using the term "Ten Commandments" Scripture scholars use the term "Decalogue," which means "the ten words."[1] This term comes from Exodus 34:28, which translated literally says that Moses "wrote on the tablets the words of the covenant, the ten utterances."

While the commandments themselves are clearly directive, telling us what to do and what not to do, the underlying theme is one of *teaching*. In the Ten Commandments, in effect, God shares divine wisdom with his people. Each commandment is a divine "word," or "utterance" spoken for our benefit. God's intention is not to order us around like slaves. Rather, the purpose of the Ten Commandments is to help us see what is good for us and what is not good for us.

In Deuteronomy, Moses speaks words that place the Ten Commandments in their proper context, making clear that the purpose of the "words" or "utterances" is to enlighten us:

> See, I have set before you today life and prosperity, death and adversity. If you obey the commandments of the LORD your God that I am commanding you today, by loving the LORD your God, walking in his ways, and observing his commandments, decrees, and ordinances, then you shall live and become

numerous, and the LORD your God will bless you in the land that you are entering to possess. But if your heart turns away and you do not hear, but are led astray to bow down to other gods and serve them, I declare to you today that you shall perish; you shall not live long in the land that you are crossing the Jordan to enter and possess. I call heaven and earth to witness against you today that I have set before you life and death, blessings and curses. Choose life so that you and your descendants may live, loving the LORD your God, obeying him, and holding fast to him; for that means life to you and length of days, so that you may live in the land that the LORD swore to give to your ancestors, to Abraham, to Isaac, and to Jacob (Deut 30:15–20).

Notice that God does not say, "Either you obey my commandments or else I will punish you severely for your disobedience." Rather, it's as if God says, "This is the natural order of things; this is how you are put together. This is the way of human nature. If you follow the utterances I give, you will thrive. If you ignore what I say, the natural consequence will be a world of hurt. The choice is yours. 'Choose life'" (Deut 30:19b).

With the Ten Commandments, then, God does not threaten us with a list of blunt rules and regulations designed to fence us in or prevent us from having any fun. Quite the opposite. G. K. Chesterton illustrates the point, quotable as he always is:

> …the curtness of the Commandments is an evidence, not of the gloom and narrowness of a religion, but, on the contrary, of its liberality and humanity. It is shorter to state the things forbidden than the things

permitted; precisely because most things are permitted, and only a few things are forbidden....It is better to tell a man not to steal than to try to tell him the thousand things that he can enjoy without stealing; especially as he can generally be pretty well trusted to enjoy them."[2]

The purpose of the Ten Commandments is to enlighten and guide, to help us act in ways that are good for us and will help us to have a life worth living.

Note that different religious traditions enumerate the commandments in slightly different ways. Jews, Roman Catholics, and Lutherans combine worshiping other Gods and making images of God into one commandment. The Orthodox and Reformed traditions separate these two as the first two commandments. Also, Jews use all of Exodus 20:2 as the first commandment: "I am the LORD your God, who brought you out of the land of Egypt, out of the house of slavery" (Ex 20:2).

The ninth and tenth commandments for Roman Catholics and Lutherans are the two prohibitions of coveting: the household (Commandment 9) and the remainder of the list in Exodus 20:17 about not coveting anything that belongs to your neighbor (Commandment 10). The contents of the Ten Commandments are the same for all Jews and Christians, however, in spite of the differences in enumeration.

A FINAL NOTE

When we read the Ten Commandments as Christians, we need to recall that Jesus had something to say on the topic, too. He adds something to the commandments.

In Matthew's Gospel, when the rich young man asks Jesus what he must do to have eternal life, Jesus first tells him to keep the commandments, but he quotes only five of them. Then, when the young man says that he already does this, Jesus replies: "If you wish to be perfect, go, sell your possessions, and give the money to the poor, and you will have treasure in heaven; then come, follow me" (Mt 19:21).

In other words, following Christ includes keeping the Ten Commandments. In addition, however, we are to follow him even at the cost of possessions and personal security. Further, Jesus makes it clear that there is a commandment that is greater than all the rest and, indeed, includes all the others:

> One of the scribes came near and heard [Jesus and some Sadducees] disputing with one another, and seeing that [Jesus] answered them well, he asked him, "Which commandment is the first of all?" Jesus answered, "The first is, 'Hear, O Israel: the Lord our God, the Lord is one; you shall love the Lord your God with all your heart, and with all your soul, and with all your mind, and with all your strength.' The second is this, 'You shall love your neighbor as yourself.' There is no other commandment greater than these" (Mk 12:28–31).

Notice that neither of the commandments that Jesus quotes is from the actual list of the Ten Commandments. The commandment to love God with your whole self comes immediately after the list of ten in Deuteronomy 6:5. The commandment to love your neighbor is in Leviticus 19:18.

For Christians, then, the Ten Commandments remain an essential source of divinely inspired moral and spiritual wisdom. Since they express our most basic duties towards God and neighbor, says the *Catechism of the Catholic Church*:

...the Ten Commandments reveal, in their primordial content, *grave* obligations. They are fundamentally immutable, and they oblige always and everywhere. No one can dispense from them. The Ten Commandments are engraved by God in the human heart."[3]

Notes

1. Bruce M. Metzger and Michael D. Coogan, eds., *The Oxford Companion to the Bible* (New York: Oxford University Press, 1993), 736. See also the *Catechism of the Catholic Church*, n. 2056: "The word *Decalogue* means literally 'ten words.'"
2. George J. Marlin, et al., eds., *More Quotable Chesterton* (San Francisco: Ignatius Press, 1988), 494.
3. See also *The Oxford Companion to the Bible*, 737. *Catechism of the Catholic Church*, n. 2072.

Chapter 1

THE TEN COMMANDMENTS IN CONTEXT

The Ten Commandments did not drop down out of heaven complete, unrelated to anything else. They are part of the revelation given to ancient Israel and preserved in the Hebrew Scriptures, or Old Testament. In fact, there are two versions of the Ten Commandments, one in the Book of Exodus (20:2–17), the other in the Book of Deuteronomy (5:6–21). Traditionally, catechetical resources conflate these two virtually identical lists into the wording of the Ten Commandments with which we are most familiar.

For example, here is how the First Commandment appears in Exodus, Deuteronomy, and a typical catechetical formulation:

Exodus 20:2–6

I am the LORD your God, who brought you out of the land of Egypt, out of the house of slavery; you shall have no other gods before me.

You shall not make for yourself an idol, whether in the form of anything that is in heaven above, or that is on the earth beneath, or that is in the water under the earth. You shall not bow down to them or worship them; for I the LORD your God am a jealous God, punishing children for the iniquity of parents, to the third and the fourth generation of those who reject me, but showing steadfast love to the thousandth generation of those who love me and keep my commandments.

Deuteronomy 5:6–10

I am the LORD your God, who brought you out of the land of Egypt, out of the house of slavery; you shall have no other gods before me.

You shall not make for yourself an idol, whether in the form of anything that is in heaven above, or that is on the earth beneath, or that is in the water under the earth. You shall not bow down to them or worship them; for I the LORD your God am a jealous God, punishing children for the iniquity of parents, to the third and fourth generation of those who reject me, but showing steadfast love to the thousandth generation of those who love me and keep my commandments.

Catechetical Formulation

I am the Lord your God: you shall not have strange gods before me.

In other words, the usual formulation of the Ten Commandments is a summary paraphrase of the actual wording in the Bible. It makes sense, therefore, that some research on the original biblical texts may yield helpful insights into the meaning of the Ten Commandments not apparent in the catechetical formula.

Be reassured that the objective is not to plow through a dry-as-dust, put-you-to-sleep-fast, exegetical excavation of the texts. Rather, we will simply read through the texts in Exodus and Deuteronomy and see what meanings there may be in any differences we find. Then, we will consult some of the usual resources to see if we can find anything noteworthy there. Finally, we will indulge ourselves in any concluding reflections that may seem appropriate.

TWO VERSIONS OF THE TEN COMMANDMENTS

If you read quickly through Exodus 20:2–17 and Deuteronomy 5:6–21, chances are you will conclude that the two versions of the Ten Commandments are identical. Take a closer look, however, and you will notice some minor differences.

Exodus and Deuteronomy give slightly different reasons for observance of the Sabbath. The former simply directs Israel to "Remember the sabbath, and keep it holy." The latter adds that this is to be done because "the Lord your God commanded you."

In the last commandment, Deuteronomy places the neighbor's wife before the neighbor's house among the things Israel is to not covet. That is the extent of the differences between the two versions.

Essentially, what we have in the Ten Commandments is a short list of religious and ethical requirements given by

God to the people of ancient Israel. This list continues to carry special authority for both Jews and Christians—and sometimes for people who are but vaguely religious—of our own time.

HOW THE COMMANDMENTS ARE ORGANIZED

If we examine the way the commandments are structured, we see that they are in four groups. The first three commandments—to worship God alone, against idol worship, and against the use of God's name for harmful reasons—emphasize God's exclusivity. That is, God has a claim on his people that no other authority may challenge.

> God will brook no rivalry; as Israel's savior, God demands a commitment that preserves the people from divided loyalties, protects them from supposing that anything in the whole of creation could adequately represent the Deity, the Creator of all, and also protects persons from the religious community's misuse of divine power to serve its own ends.[1]

The second group of commandments consists of two that call Israel to set aside every seventh day as a day free from work, and to honor parents—with the implication that this is particularly important when parents grow old. These two commandments address basic social needs, namely, the human need for leisure and rest and the need to preserve human dignity against abuse or exploitation even when people are no longer able to be "productive" members of the community.

Three commandments that target the individual and the family in the context of the larger community make up the third group. These commandments insist on the holiness of human life, the holiness of marriage and of the sexual expression of marriage, and the need to maintain a community that respects the individual's rights of ownership.

The final group consists of two commandments that deal with issues that are social and public. They require people to speak truthfully in court or before the elders of the community. They also call for living a life free from a craving to possess anyone else's goods or life.

MOSES: THE GREAT LAWGIVER

Behind the Ten Commandments stands the monumental figure of Moses, the liberator and lawgiver. It was through Moses that God freed the Israelites from slavery in Egypt, and it was through Moses that God gave Israel the Ten Commandments. It is the consensus among modern Scripture scholars that the substance of the Ten Commandments did originate with Moses.[2]

The condemnation of idolatry in the Ten Commandments and the requirement that one day each week be observed as the Sabbath—a day when normal occupations and concerns are set aside—are unique in ancient Near Eastern societies and cultures. The other commandments are not unique, but this collection of ten short, basically negative, commandments is unique. "It stems from a person of extraordinary religious discernment—and Moses was such a person."[3]

It is likely that the Ten Commandments originated with a close connection to family life. Such a concise list would have been an ideal way for parents to teach their children the basic requirements of the covenant between God and Israel. They also probably had a regular place in the religious life of the community and in the great festivals when the covenant was celebrated and reaffirmed.

It may also be no accident that there are ten, not nine and not eleven, commandments. This made the "words" or "utterances" easy to remember by counting them off on the ten fingers of the hands. The fact that the Ten Commandments are basically negative in character should not be misinterpreted as coming from a grim God. Rather, it is more likely that the negative slant to the commandments was intended to shape the people's understanding of the kinds of behavior that would, automatically, destroy community life and so had to be forbidden.

The original purpose of the Ten Commandments was not legalistic. Instead, they were meant to prevent behaviors among the people that could lead to the destruction of the community. The intention was not to hamstring people with oppressive legalisms. Rather, the goal was to call the Israelites to a life liberated to flourish in community. In a very real sense, the Ten Commandments constitute the foundation for a lasting community life.

With all this in mind, then, we move along to look at each of the Ten Commandments in greater depth and detail to see what meaning each may have for today.

Notes

1. Walter Harrelson, "Ten Commandments" in Bruce M. Metzger and Michael D. Coogan, eds., *The Oxford Companion to the Bible* (New York: Oxford University Press, 1993), 737.
2. See Harrelson, 737.
3. Harrelson, 737.

Chapter 2

THE FIRST COMMANDMENT

Catechetical Formula

I am the LORD your God: you shall not have strange gods before me.

Scriptural Version

I am the LORD your God, who brought you out of the land of Egypt, out of the house of slavery; you shall have no other gods before me.

You shall not make for yourself an idol, whether in the form of anything that is in heaven above, or that is on the earth beneath, or that is in the water under the earth. You shall not bow down to them or worship them....

EXODUS 20:2–5

I magine you are the subject of an unexpected television interview. There you are in a mall or walking through a supermarket minding your own business, when suddenly a television interviewer sticks a microphone in your face.

"Have you ever worshiped an idol?" the interviewer asks, a smile pasted in place. "We're doing a random set of interviews, and we'd like to know. Have you ever worshiped an idol?"

If you are like most people, you would be incredulous. "Have I what?" you might stammer, glancing nervously at the camera perched on the camera operator's shoulder.

"Have you ever worshiped an idol? You know, a false god?"

Finally, gathering your wits together, you reply with an embarrassed little laugh, "No. No, of course not. Don't be ridiculous."

This is how most of us would reply to such a question. In our culture, the idea of idol worship is considered silly. Who would be stupid enough to actually worship a statue or other image? Maybe so, but let's take a look at the meaning of the key words here, *idol* and *worship*. According to one dictionary, an idol is "an image used as an object of worship; a false god." According to the same dictionary, "worship" is: "1. The reverent love and devotion accorded a deity, an idol, or a sacred object. The ceremonies, prayers, or other religious forms by which this love is expressed. 2. Ardent devotion; adoration."[1]

When the television interviewer asks you if you have ever worshiped an idol, you probably think of a statue, maybe even the golden calf worshiped by the Israelites in the desert (Ex 32:4–8). What nonsense, you think. Nobody would worship a statue today. Certainly not me. The key phrase in the definition given above, however, is "a false god." Now we are down to brass tacks. A "false god" is another thing entirely because a false god need not be a statue or other image.

You would need to poke around in a large number of garage or yard sales to find a statue worthy of being an idol, but to find a false god all you need do is open your morning newspaper or switch on a television or radio. You got false gods, I got false gods, all God's children got false gods in abundance. We worship them daily. Without even knowing it, we worship false gods by the dozen. Of course, none of them are statues or images. They are all abstractions.

THE FALSE GOD OF FINANCIAL SECURITY

One of the most popular false gods in the so-called developed Western nations is the false god called Financial Security. Before you protest, first allow me to say that there is absolutely nothing wrong with wanting to have an adequate income and provide for your retirement years. Where Financial Security becomes a false god is when we begin to believe that there is no such thing as too much financial security.

Remember what Jesus says in Matthew's Gospel: "Do not store up for yourselves treasures on earth, where moth and rust consume and where thieves break in and steal; but store up for yourselves treasures in heaven, where neither moth nor rust consumes and where thieves do not break in and steal" (6:19–20).

And: "No one can serve two masters; for a slave will either hate the one and love the other, or be devoted to the one and despise the other. You cannot serve God and wealth" (Mt 6:24).

Had someone strolled up to Jesus one day and asked

him to explain the First Commandment, he might have used these same words. Jesus had a bad feeling about earthly treasures and wealth, and the reason he had a bad feeling about them was that it is so easy for earthly wealth to become a substitute for God—in other words, a false god. It is so easy to trust in bank accounts, mutual funds, certificates of deposit, investments, insurance policies, and the like, instead of trusting in God.

We are adept at saying one thing and doing another. We find it easy to give lip service to trust in God, then turn around and give our heart to a money market account.

There are even sectarian Christian authors who write books that celebrate the idea that, by golly, God wants you to be richer than Solomon. Not only that, such authors insist, but if you are "a good Christian" you can't help but be wealthy because true faith leads to wealth. Pardon me if I think Jesus would reply to such authors, "And just which gospel is it you're talking about? It certainly isn't the gospel *I'm* talking about. The good news I bring has nothing to do with hauling in money."

Does this mean that wealthy people can't possibly be good Christians? Of course not, but it does mean that Jesus isn't kidding when he says that it's not easy for rich folks to enter the kingdom of God. Take a look at this exchange from the Gospel of Mark:

> Then Jesus looked around and said to his disciples, "How hard it will be for those who have wealth to enter the kingdom of God!" And the disciples were perplexed at these words. But Jesus said to them again, "Children, how hard it is to enter the kingdom of God! It is easier for a camel to go through the eye of a needle than for someone who is rich to enter the kingdom of God." They were greatly astounded

and said to one another, "Then who can be saved?" Jesus looked at them and said, "For mortals it is impossible, but not for God; for God all things are possible" (Mk 10:23–27).

Notice what happens here. Jesus does not say that a rich person cannot be his disciple. He does not say that rich people cannot enter the kingdom of God. He simply and straightforwardly declares that it's not impossible for wealthy people to live lives of authentic faith. God, for whom "all things are possible," can save such people. Jesus makes it clear, however, that it's easy for wealth to be a serious threat to one's eternal destiny. Wealthy people had better take extra precautions, that's all. Wealthy people need to use their wealth in ways that are helpful to others.

In other words, idol worship is a major stumbling block for the wealthy, and the false god they need to be on the lookout for is financial forms of security. One of the best examples of how money can get a grip on the human heart and turn into a false god appears in one of the great works of nineteenth-century English literature, *Silas Marner: The Weaver of Raveloe*, by George Eliot (Mary Ann Evans). Early in the story, Silas Marner is the victim of a great injustice, and as a result he becomes reclusive and self-centered. Accumulating money becomes his only passion:

He began to think [the money] was conscious of him, as his loom was, and he would on no account have exchanged those coins, which had become his familiars, for other coins with unknown faces. He handled them, he counted them, till their form and colour were like the satisfaction of a thirst to him; but it was only in the night, when his work was done, that he drew them out to enjoy their companionship. He had taken up some bricks in his floor underneath his loom, and here he had made a hole in which he set the iron pot that contained his guineas and silver coins, covering the bricks with sand whenever he replaced them.[2]

Although *Silas Marner* is the story of a conversion and the redemptive power of love, at this early stage in the story Silas Marner is a man who loves money, who *worships* money. He accumulates money for its own sake and for the sake of the emotional, even spiritual, security he imagines he gets from it. At night, he takes out his gold and silver coins to "enjoy their companionship" with no thought of how he could use his wealth to help others.

As with all the Ten Commandments, the First Commandment is for the sake of our greater spiritual freedom, not for the sake of fencing us in. Popular opinion would have us believe that the more money we have, and the more financial security we have, the happier we will be. We all need a certain level of income, of course, and there are all kinds of financial planning strategies that are prudent and good. But the point of the First Commandment, when it comes to money, is that there are limits.

There are people who have annual incomes that are obscene: the CEOs of certain megacorporations, for example, who pull down hundreds of millions of dollars a year. Does anyone really need that much money? One might say that such incomes cry to heaven for vengeance, unless, of course, the person who has it gives it away. Otherwise, we are talking about first-class idol worship. Of course, it is possible that people who receive annual paychecks in the millions could be doing much good with their money, but if they are most of them do a great job of keeping it a secret.

"THE PROTESTANT PRINCIPLE"

The First Commandment is about more than the worship of money, of course. Ultimately, it is about giving our heart to anything other than the true God. Whenever we care more about anything than we do about the love of God, we are in conflict with the First Commandment.

Although it may come as a bit of a surprise to Catholics, the First Commandment is about what theologian Paul Tillich called "the Protestant Principle." Even though this principle was central to the Protestant Reformation, it is basic to Christianity—indeed, to all great religions—in whatever form.[3] Essentially, this principle says that only God is God.

Stated negatively, the Protestant Principle objects to "any absolute claim made for a finite reality, whether it be a church, a book, a symbol, a person, or an event."[4] Stated positively, this principle insists that "grace is not bound to any finite form, that God is the inexhaustible power and ground of all being, and that the truest faith is just that one which has an element of self-negation in it because it points beyond itself to that which is really ultimate."[5] In other words, to repeat, only God is God.

One of the ways the First Commandment and the Protestant Principle come in handy in a Catholic context is to help us keep the sacraments in perspective. A sacrament, to quote Saint Augustine, is "a visible sign of an invisible reality." The sacrament of the Eucharist, for example, carries the real presence of the risen Christ. But even a sacrament is not God. A sacrament is a means to an end, not an end in itself. So even when we pray before the Blessed Sacrament we pray to Christ present in the sacrament, not to the sacrament itself.

CULTIVATING A PERSONAL
RELATIONSHIP WITH CHRIST

Another way in which the First Commandment may be applied is in human relationships. When you observe the First Commandment, you do not give undue credit or power to the opinions of others. You do not live your life according to the expectations of other people or in order to be liked and accepted by others. Rather, you try to live according to the gospel and the will of God in your life.

The First Commandment is, ultimately, about having a faith that is authentic and having your priorities in order. Faith may be defined in several ways, but the essence of Christian faith is personal intimacy with Christ and an ongoing relationship with the Body of Christ, the people of God, the Church. Consequently, the most effective way to observe the First Commandment is to cultivate your relationship with Christ and with the Church. By "Church," of course, we mean both your local Catholic parish community and the worldwide Catholic Church community, which cannot be separated from each other.

The best way to avoid hanky-panky with false gods is to maintain a healthy focus on loving intimacy with the true God and with his people. This begs the question, however, about the ways to do this. Since we are talking about relationships—with Christ and the human faith community—the ways are easy to identify. Fundamentally, we nourish intimacy with Christ and with the Body of Christ, the people of God, and the Church by giving time and attention to those relationships.

CULTIVATING A
PERSONAL PRAYER LIFE

Of course, the ways we give time and attention to our relationships take different forms. But most of them have one thing in common. They all include the need to spend time together. As popular speaker, counselor, and author Clayton C. Barbeau is fond of saying, "Where you put your time you put your life, and where you put your life you put your love."[6] Thus, one of the essential ways you observe the First Commandment is to give some time, each day, to a form of prayer that "works" for you.

You observe the First Commandment, and avoid spiritual involvement with false gods, when you consciously turn to the true God, open yourself to his unconditional love, express your gratitude, reveal your needs, and give yourself to him in simple, honest acts of loving worship. For you, this may mean reading prayers from a book or a single prayer from a card in a wallet or a purse or simply remaining silent and open for a moment to God's loving presence. It may mean praying the rosary, or it may mean slowly praying through one of the psalms. It may mean some form of silent meditation, or for you it may be breathing a quiet prayer of petition for God's help in your busy life as you change the baby's first diaper of the day and get the older kids off to school.

It's difficult to describe prayer "in general" because prayer is as unique as each individual. Some people seem to have days as smooth as satin. Some people seem blessed with ideal children. Most of us, however, have days that are wild with activity, and most of us have children that do not fit the expectations we had before they were born. It is in this "real world" that prayer needs to happen, and what matters is *that* you pray, not *how* you pray.

For most people, prayer changes depending on what's going on in their lives. Prayer is different for unmarried people than for married people; different for people with children than for people without children or whose children are teenagers rather than toddlers. Prayer is different for parents whose kids are grown and gone than for people who just had their first baby. Prayer is sometimes different for men than for women, and prayer is often different for teenagers than it is for people who are thirty-something or fifty-something. Prayer is like life, always changing, always unpredictable, always full of surprises—some of them pleasant, some of them not.

Again, what matters is *that* you pray, not *how* you pray. Do not try to model your prayer on some highly "spiritual" ideal you heard about or read about in a book. Most likely, you are not a cloistered monk or nun. You are a "front line" Christian, and that is where your prayer will happen, in the course of your ordinary, everyday, knockabout life. Do not feel inferior because you do not measure up to an ideal that is unrealistic for you. Prayer is not a performance art. It's an act of love and adoration, and such acts are highly personal. If the way you pray seems forced and artificial, give it up. Find a way to pray that lets you be yourself with God.

Now, however, that we have given minimalism its due—and all too often minimalism with regard to prayer doesn't get the credit it deserves—it's time for an admission. Chances are, when it comes to prayer you could do better or do more. Chances are, when it comes to prayer you are like most people, a bit of a lazy bones. If you take a close look at your life, more than likely you can see ways that you could give more time to prayer.

A big part of our problem as Westerners and Christians is that typically we look at prayer as separate from life, an activity reserved for moments set aside from the world of the ordinary. We can learn a great deal about this attitude from other religious traditions such as Orthodox Judaism and Islam.[7] Orthodox Jews pray three times a day, and there are many blessings for many occasions. Devout Muslims pray five times a day in a formal, ritualistic manner, no matter where they are or what they are doing. In other words, for both Orthodox Judaism and Islam, being Jewish or Muslim makes a real difference in everyday life.

Being Catholic should make a difference in everyday life, too. It's true that Catholicism is especially sensitive to the sacred in the ordinary, but regular prayer is necessary to maintain this sensitivity. So while the minimalist approach to prayer we discussed above is valid, sometimes we could do more. Our tradition doesn't have a required built-in structure of daily prayer for lay people such as we find in Islam or Judaism; however, there are options we can turn to.

Daily Mass

One of the best options for daily prayer is also one of the most obvious, namely, daily Mass. Far more people could participate in the Eucharist on a daily basis than actually do so. Be realistic, of course. Your work schedule may make this impossible. Retired people may have the ideal situation for daily Mass attendance. Stay-at-home parents often could attend daily Mass, however, if they wanted to. If you stick your head inside just about any parish church on a weekday morning you may be surprised to see mothers or fathers there for Mass with babies and/or young children. At the very least, don't reject the idea without giving it a try or two.

The Rosary

Prayer is how we nourish union with the true God and keep ourselves free from "strange gods." Thus, it makes sense to cultivate prayer as a daily habit. A traditional devotional form of prayer that countless Christians—most but not all of them Catholics—find enriching is the rosary. Intercessory prayer to the Holy Trinity through Mary, the mother of Jesus, has this advantage: it brings you into conscious union with God in the context of the communion of saints.

Recitation of the repetitive prayers of the rosary, the feel of the beads slipping slowly through the fingers, contemplation of the Sorrowful, Joyful, and Glorious Mysteries, add up to a devotional prayer you can use in all kinds of situations. The rosary is an "all-purpose prayer," appropriate whether you are worried, happy, sad, anxious, or calm and at peace.

Liturgy of the Hours

A prayer option used by an increasing number of Catholics is the Liturgy of the Hours or some adaptation thereof. Essentially, the Liturgy of the Hours provides a set of psalms, antiphons, hymns, blessings, and other prayers organized according to the model of the monastic hours of prayer. Prayer times occur in the wee hours of the night (although only monastic communities usually get up in the very early morning hours), in the morning, at noon, in the evening, and at night before bedtime. To pray the official Liturgy of the Hours you need to invest in a rather expensive set of prayer books, but adaptations of the Liturgy of the Hours are available for considerably less. *Magnificat*, a small magazine published monthly gives you, in effect, a brief form of the Liturgy of the Hours along with the Scriptural readings for each day's Mass and other inspirational readings.[8]

If the First Commandment is an invitation to make prayer a part of your everyday life, the Liturgy of the Hours is designed to nourish your awareness of God's loving presence throughout your day. The inclination may be to say that by such prayer we "sanctify" our day. But that's not accurate. It would be more to the point to say that by prayer we nourish our awareness of the fact that God is always there, that every moment is holy, that our day is already "sanctified." It is we who need to remember this and cultivate a sensitivity to it by including prayer in our day.

EXAMINING OUR LIFESTYLE

Finally, the First Commandment has definite implications for that modern concept, our "lifestyle." If we give our heart to the true God alone, who is our loving Father, then we need to take care when it comes to the many other things that try to make a claim on our heart. Living in an affluent society means that most of us need to be concerned about this, even if we do not think of ourselves as "wealthy." Compared to the vast majority of the people on the planet, most of us are indeed wealthy. This does not mean that we need to adopt an extreme or outlandish lifestyle. It does mean that we need to take seriously our need for simplicity of life. We need to take steps to be free of our possessions so that we possess them, they do not possess us.

How you maintain some spiritual freedom from possessions is a matter for creativity on your part. No one can tell anyone else the specifics of how to use possessions in a way that leaves you free from them.

In his astonishing and delightful novel, *Mariette in Ecstasy*, Ron Hansen has the main character, Mariette, write in a letter: "*We try to be formed and held and kept by [Christ], but instead he offers us freedom. And now when I try to know his will, his kindness floods me, his great love overwhelms me, and I hear him whisper, Surprise me.*"[9]

God leaves us free to choose how we will observe not only the First Commandment, but all ten of them. What matters is *that* we live according to the commandments, not *how* we do so, and the ways are many. Certainly we can consult the example set by others. We can refer to the wisdom of saints and ordinary believers down through the centuries. We can read the works of spiritual writers and theologians. We can, and should, be guided by the wisdom of the Church found in, for example, the *Catechism of the Catholic Church* and the *Documents of Vatican II*. We need the light that comes from prayer and the sacraments. But in the long run what we hear will be a whisper in our heart saying, "Surprise me."

Notes

1. Excerpted from *American Heritage Talking Dictionary*. Copyright © 1997, The Learning Company, Inc. All Rights Reserved.
2. George Eliot, *Silas Marner* (New York: Penguin Classics, 1861/1967), 68.
3. See Van A. Harvey, *A Handbook of Theological Terms* (New York: Macmillan, 1964), 197.
4. Harvey, 197–198.
5. Harvey, 198.
6. See, for example, Clayton C. Barbeau, *Delivering the Male: Out of the Tough-Guy Trap Into a Better Marriage* (San Francisco: Ikon Press, 1982).
7. For insights into prayer as spirituality from various world religions, see Mitch Finley, *Prayer for People Who Think Too Much: A Guide to Everyday, Anywhere Prayer From the World's Faith Traditions* (Woodstock, VT: SkyLight Paths, 1999)

8. For subscription information: *Magnificat*, P.O. Box 91, Spencerville, MA 20868–9978. Phone (301) 853-6600. Fax (301) 559-5167. On the Internet, www.magnificat.net.

9. Ron Hansen, *Mariette in Ecstasy* (New York: HarperCollins, 1991), 179. Italics are in original text.

Chapter 3

THE SECOND COMMANDMENT

Catechetical Formula

You shall not take the name of the LORD your God in vain.

Scriptural Version

You shall not make wrongful use of the name of the LORD your God, for the LORD will not acquit anyone who misuses his name.

EXODUS 20:7

Without a doubt, the most commonly misunderstood commandment is this one. The Second Commandment, *in its original meaning*, does *not* forbid the use of "God" as an exclamatory remark. It doesn't even forbid the use of profanity or "swearing." Say you are driving a nail into a board, and you accidentally hit your thumb with the hammer. You drop the hammer, and as you dance around holding your injured thumb you shout an expletive that uses God's name as part of an idiom. You did not "break" the Second Commandment. Your thumb, maybe, but not the Second Commandment. You may have violated good manners, but you did not violate the law of God.

The above translation of Exodus 20:7 abandons the term "in vain" in favor of "wrongful use," but this still leaves room for misunderstanding. To do something—anything—"in vain," means to do so uselessly or to no avail. The original meaning of the Second Commandment is best understood in a legal context. "The prohibition seems to be against the false use of an oath in legal proceedings rather than a general lack of reverence for the name."[1]

Recall that for the ancient Israelites there was no separation between sacred and secular, between holy and profane. Neither the ancient Israelites nor the Hebrew Scriptures share our modern dichotomy between religion and the ordinary. For the authors of the book of Exodus, religion and culture are one. So it makes perfect sense that a legal context is not a "secular" context, as it is for us "enlightened" moderns. Rather, a legal situation for the ancient Israelites was just as religious as any other. Therefore, it would be important for them to insist that it is not acceptable to call on God to witness your words and then speak anything but the truth. This is what the Second Commandment was all about in its original meaning.

This does not mean that, here and now, habitual "swearing" and profanity are perfectly fine. In fact, in our time the use of crude and offensive language has gone way beyond "taking the name of the LORD your God in vain." These days, if the only way you hear God's name profaned is in a great many movies, you may consider yourself fortunate, indeed. Sometimes you can't help but get the impression—

especially from movies—that many people today are incapable of expressing strong feelings or convictions without using a stream of cursing, profanity, and suggestions that other people are anatomically malformed, punctuated by crude gestures and insults to the institution of the family.

Perhaps this should come as no surprise, given the constantly descending level of cultural values in general. Being crude and offensive seems almost to be the "in thing." What can you do when the automobile ahead of you in traffic, driven by a complete stranger, carries a bumper sticker that is crude and offensive and/or insults your intelligence?

All this is unfortunate and sad, but you can't appeal to the Second Commandment, as it was originally intended in the Book of Exodus, to encourage more polite or respectful forms of expression and behavior. Admirable as such a goal would certainly be, this was simply not the meaning of the Second Commandment in the context of ancient Israel. We may wonder, then, why a prohibition of "the false use of an oath in legal proceedings" was so important that it became one of the Ten Commandments. We may also wonder—since it's not about foul language—what is the Second Commandment about today.

Here we have an excellent example of why both Scripture *and* Tradition constitute a unified source of divine revelation. If we limit ourselves strictly to the scriptural meaning of the Second Commandment, we can go no further than we already have gone. Once we open the door to Tradition, however, we see that this commandment has a much wider application than its literal, historical meaning. We discover that the Second Commandment has several meanings.

A WIDER MEANING

First, if we reflect on the meaning of the Second Commandment we see that its first, most basic, meaning is to remind us that the divine name is holy. The *Catechism of the Catholic Church* (n. 2142), one expression of Sacred Tradition, teaches that the Second Commandment is about showing respect for the divine and the holy. It is about how we speak about sacred matters. In other words, when we consciously speak about God, Jesus, and even Mary and the saints, the rule is one of respect, all day, every day.

In a moment of pain or justifiable anger, say, you may give out with an inappropriate reference to God, but this is not an intentional religious reference. It is nothing more than a secular, culturally rooted expression of pain or anger. Of course, we should always guard against letting a phrase such as this one become a habit. Most people find habitual swearing, cursing, and profanity offensive. The habitual use of God's name in disrespectful ways is a symptom of a weak or unhealthy spirituality. If our faith, our loving intimacy with God, with Jesus, with Mary and the saints is healthy and alive, we will naturally avoid abusing these names, just as we would avoid the disrespectful use of the names of anyone we love and care for.

If you claim to be a Christian, yet your everyday speech mannerisms include the thoughtless, disrespectful use of sacred names, others are not likely to be impressed with your claim to be a religious person. This includes the thoughtless invocation of God's name when making a promise to another person, as in "I swear to God I'll pay you back next week." If you say something like this, you should not say it lightly or merely as a way to pressure the other person into doing what you want.

INTERPERSONAL RELATIONSHIPS

Your relationship with God cannot be separated from your relationships with other people, and the Second Commandment is a good illustration of this. The Second Commandment appears to be entirely about our relationship with God; but, in fact, it is also about our relationships with one another. In its original scriptural meaning, the Second Commandment insists that we not use God's name to give false witness in a legal context. Clearly, even if we limit ourselves to this original meaning there is also a social aspect. In legal and everyday situations, we are to be truthful in our dealings with other people.

Once we include the wisdom of Sacred Tradition, however, the interpersonal dimension of the Second Commandment becomes even more evident. When we choose to not use sacred names in disrespectful ways, we also choose to show respect for other people. For almost invariably, other people are present if we show disrespect for the name of God, or Jesus, and they will be offended, perhaps even scandalized.

What do we choose when we choose to observe the Second Commandment in its fullness, as presented to us in the context of both Scripture and Sacred Tradition? We choose to overcome, if only a little, the sacred/secular dichotomy that so radically characterizes modern Western cultures. When we choose to not "make wrongful use" of the name of God, of Jesus, of Mary, and of the saints, we choose to inhabit a universe where the sacred is one with the ordinary, where we would no more "make wrongful use" of sacred names than we would "make wrongful use" of the names of our loved ones. For God, Jesus, Mary, and the saints are "loved ones," too.

This is no small point. Theologian Craig M. Gay summarizes a modern assumption:

...one of the most consequential ideas embedded in modern institutions and traditions and habits of thought is theological. Stated bluntly, it is the assumption that even if God does exist he is largely irrelevant to the real business of life. To put this somewhat more tactfully, contemporary society and culture so emphasize human potential and human agency and the immediate practical exigencies of the here and now, that we are for the most part tempted to go about our daily business in this world without giving God much thought. Indeed, we are tempted to live as though God did not exist, or at least as if his existence did not practically matter.[2]

To avoid using sacred names in profane ways is not a sign that you are a puritanical prude. Rather, when we choose to observe the Second Commandment in all its fullness we choose to live—by the ways we express ourselves verbally—as though God *does* exist and *does* matter to the concerns of our ordinary, everyday life. Indeed, from a distinctively Catholic perspective we choose to live as if God is *inseparable* from ordinary, everyday life. God, the risen Christ, the Blessed Mother, and all the saints *are real*, and they are *present, here and now*. Therefore, we show respect for all that is sacred by not misusing the sacred names. Not only that, but there is something to the old observation that only people with a weak vocabulary find it necessary to swear, curse, and use profanity in a casual, habitual manner.

CULTURAL OBSTACLES

The biggest obstacle to observance of the Second Commandment has already been mentioned, and it is not one we can easily dismiss. That obstacle is living in a culture that drives a wedge between religion and life, between the sacred and the secular, between the holy and the everyday. This situation exists; it is a fact of life. But when you choose to avoid profaning—which means showing irreverence or contempt for God—the sacred names, then you choose to transcend the sacred/secular dichotomy and bring them back together, at least a little, in your own life.

In a very real sense, to observe the Second Commandment is to admit publicly that you are not the center of the universe, that there are transcendent Realities much bigger and more important than yourself—Realities too holy to be profaned. To observe the Second Commandment is to preserve certain words and ideas for use only in solemn and sacred situations.

Vows and promises made to others in God's name become cheapened when we use the same, or similar, words for trivial for superficial reasons. When a man and woman marry, they make vows to each other in God's name. They invoke God's divine fidelity and truthfulness to witness and preserve their marital union. If then, in their everyday lives, this same man and woman make a habit of using God's name in "wrongful" ways, that would detract from or cheapen or even subtly nullify the way in which they invoked God's name when they recited their marriage vows. We need to be careful about how we use sacred names because we need those names to retain the rightful power and authority they have when used in appropriate ways.

To act in ways contrary to the Second Commandment may even weaken your faith and your belief in the reality of

God's love for you. To use God's name in profane ways is to neutralize it so that when you use that same name in explicitly religious contexts, at prayer, in the liturgy, and so forth, it has lost some of its power and meaning. To refer to God in profane ways is to short-circuit his reality for you when what you need, in today's world, is a deeper sense of God, not a shallower one.

Sheila Cassidy is an Oxford-trained English physician and director of a hospice for the terminally ill. She says that what allows her to be at ease with death and dying is her deeply felt belief in God:

> I have such a deep gut level belief in God and in the afterlife that I can, if you like, cock a snoot at death, that I can look death in the eye and be at ease with the dying. It's not that I know that I wouldn't be personally frightened if I knew that I had cancer, because I would, but there's a very real sense in which I believe that this life is a pilgrimage and that the next life is where we're going. And although I'm sad, sad for people who suffer, sad for people who have to face death, I don't see death as a tragedy at all. I mean, I was thinking this morning, I don't give a fig if I die now, today, tomorrow. It just doesn't matter because I believe that our life is in God, and I really believe that, like I believe in having breakfast. It's not on an intellectual level. And so if your belief in God and your experience of God in prayer actually gets to that level of your guts, then it means that you behave in a different way to people.[3]

One of the ways we can have this gut-level belief in God is to observe the Second Commandment, by refusing to refer to God as if God is nothing but an abstraction or theory.

If God is real and God the Creator and God is love—as the Gospel of John declares—then what sense does it make to speak of him in any but respectful terms?

A CULTURAL LENS

We began this chapter by insisting that it was not the original intent of the authors of Exodus to present the Second Commandment as forbidding the use of God's name in swearing or profanity. Yet we have spent considerable effort discussing just that. This is because for all practical purposes the original legal meaning of the Second Commandment has no contemporary relevance. Therefore, we are left with the secondary meaning of this commandment, which covers our need to act as if God is a loving God who is real and present.

One of the most intriguing ways to examine the Second Commandment today is through the lens of popular culture. By this I mean the work of writers, musicians, artists, filmmakers, anyone who contributes in a noticeable way to the dominant cultural ethos, the cultural environment in which contemporary people live and move like a fish swims in water. Sometimes the popular culture addresses the reality, or unreality, of God explicitly. At other times, it does so in a thoroughly secular, even profane, manner. But the issue is the same, namely, the reality or unreality of God. And the underlying question is "Does the Second Commandment make sense today?"

Another way to express this issue is to pose the question of God's presence in the ordinary. If God is present in the mundane everyday world, then the Second Commandment makes sense. If God is not present in the everyday, then it does not make sense. It is astonishing how often contributors to contemporary culture respond to this question in the affirmative. Let's take a look at a few examples, each one showing us a world where the Second Commandment is right at home.

Stevie Smith (1902–1971): Relishing the Divine Mystery

English poet Stevie Smith's work sometimes addresses religious issues in ways that eschew conventional piety. At the same time, rather than rejecting organized religion, Smith asks religion to take more seriously the incomprehensibility of God. She asks the reader to be honest about his or her predominant image of God and not use such images to neutralize the divine. She says, in effect, that the Second Commandment is important because it preserves both God's immanence—God's presence with us—and God's transcendence—God's "beyondness."

In her poem "God Speaks," Stevie Smith presents a God who, to the shock of conventional Christian theology and piety, makes mistakes. At the same time, the God who "speaks" in this poem is a God who loves all creatures: "I made Man with too many faults. Yet I love him. / And if he wishes, I have a home above for him."

Smith's God insists that he wants "Man" to be happy. Indeed, God insists on his own geniality. Then the poem gives a poke in the eye to a common but skewed Christian theology of redemption. God insists on not being portrayed "as if I were abominable," for example, "that I had a son and gave him for their salvation" (that is, like a sacrifical animal). Thinking of God in this way is one of the faults of humans: "It leads to nervous prostration." When we observe the Second Commandment, however, we preserve an awareness of God's reality.

God eventually wants people to be happy with him in

heaven, but there is a "difficulty." People can be "home" with God later only "by being already at home here."[4]

In a few brief lines of poetry, Stevie Smith shakes up the believer's safe, secure religious world, saying in effect that it is important for God to remain, above all, the Divine Mystery and ultimately be impossible to pin down. Those who, on the contrary, ignore the Second Commandment and refer to God in trivial or disrespectful ways imply that God is easy to pin down because God is an illusion.

In another poem, "Egocentric," Smith boldly asks a question that haunts many believers but which most never ask: "What care I if Skies are blue, / If God created Gnat and Gnu, / What care I if good God be / If He be not good to me?"[5]

Yet another of Stevie Smith's poems, "Oh Christianity, Christianity," gently flogs conventional Christian religion for sidestepping questions that nag many people including the poet herself: "Oh Christianity, Christianity, / Why do you not answer our difficulties?... // You say, Christianity, you say / That the Trinity is unchanging from eternity,/ but then you say / At the incarnation He took / Our Manhood into the Godhead, / that did not have it before, / so it must have altered it, / Having it. // Oh what do you mean, what do you mean? / You never answer our questions."[6]

To read poems such as these is to find yourself faced with the need to understand and admit the limits of religious language, metaphors, and analogies, to admit that all religious language attempts to talk about a God who cannot be captured by the human intellect. To make such an admission is, of course, to situate yourself for intimacy with God, and the truth behind the Second Commandment becomes unquestionable.

Vincent Van Gogh (1853-1890): Enraptured by Transcendence

Vincent Van Gogh may not seem contemporary, but he anticipated by several decades the modern perspective. Van Gogh's religious background was evangelical Christian, and he even tried for a time to become a minister. For years before his suicide—brought about by mental illness—Vincent portrayed in his paintings his perception of the Divine Mystery present in both people and nature. Famous paintings, such as "Sunflowers" and "The Starry Night," reveal the divine presence in the earth and in the universe that Vincent saw and felt in a most profound and joyful manner. Lesser known works, such as "Girl Kneeling in Front of a Cradle" and "The Potato Eaters," communicate the mystery of human existence including both its light and dark sides.

To gain more specific insights into the mind of Van Gogh, however, we may turn to his hundreds of letters, in which he often discussed religious and spiritual ideas. Vincent's image of God is, of course, basic to both his painting and his religious concepts. According to one commentator, "Vincent came to view the 'flaws' and 'flimsiness' of creation as evidence that God is a daring Artist who always attempts more than He can do, thus promising greater works as the total 'oeuvre' unfolds."[7]

Vincent saw in the imperfect world proof for God's existence, not the opposite. Thus he suggests that the Second Commandment is far from irrelevant to everyday life.

> ...the study is ruined in so many ways. It is only a master who can make such a blunder, and perhaps that is the best consolation we can have out of it, since in that case we have a right to hope that we'll see the same creative hand get even with itself.[8]

Through prayer, Van Gogh sought to unite himself and his efforts as an artist with the Artist. In this way, Vincent teaches that much can be learned by anyone who would look to his or her own work as a way to understand God. Prayer and spirituality become not something aside from everyday life but the full expression of the sacred present in the ordinary. And in this ordinary world, the Second Commandment bids us speak of God with respect and reverence.

Yet Van Gogh's spirituality would not allow him to fixate on any single image of God. Because of what he saw in creation, his deepest convictions were of God's utter transcendence, a classically Protestant world view. As he wrote to his brother, Theo:

> ...but I love, and how could I feel love if I did not live and others did not live; and then if we live, there is something mysterious in that. Now call it God or human nature or whatever you like, but there is something which I cannot define systematically, though it is very much alive and very real, and see that is God, or as good as God.[9]

Shusaku Endo (1923-1997): The Courage to Be Catholic

Shusaku Endo was a Japanese novelist who as a boy converted to Catholicism, a religion that has many connections with Western culture. Endo's fiction frequently deals with the clash between Western and Japanese culture. All of his novels—including *Silence*, *The Sea and Poison*, *Volcano*, *The Samurai*, *When I Whistle*, and *Deep River*—illustrate how difficult it is for the Japanese to assimilate Christianity. All the same, Endo's novels have attracted more than a few converts to Christianity. For Westerners, Endo's novels can enrich the sense of God's presence in the everyday and reinforce the value of always speaking of the sacred in appropriate ways.

One of the best examples of Shusaku Endo's understanding of authentic faith appears in Gaston Bonaparte, the main character in an early novel, *Wonderful Fool*.[10] Gaston is a bumbling, physically unattractive, but likable young Frenchman who arrives in Tokyo with a mission on his mind. He is irresistibly attracted to victims of all kinds and the downtrodden of Japanese society. Gaston adopts a stray mongrel dog and rescues a good-hearted prostitute and thief. He enjoys hanging around with an old hermit fortuneteller. Finally, Gaston befriends a wild-eyed, cold-blooded killer who becomes the ultimate challenge to his compassion.

Gaston is a Christ-figure who ignores the standards and values of practical society in favor of giving himself in service to those who most need such attention—whether they appreciate it or not. In the end, Gaston dies for his commitment—or does he? The final words of the novel only highlight Gaston's mysterious status as a Christ-figure: "Gaston is still alive. One day he'll come lumbering down again from that far-off azure country to take back once more the sorrow of people like these."[11]

From Shusaku Endo's fiction, those who strive to cultivate the spirit of prayer and keep their religion alive can learn what courage it takes to do that in a culture antagonistic to what lies deepest in the believer's heart. From *Wonderful Fool*, in particular, those who would know the purpose of faith in God can learn that faith is anything but peripheral to everyday life and real people. They can learn of the sacrifices required by authentic faith. They can learn that to observe the Second Commandment is to admit God into one's everyday life.

Stella Gibbons (1920-1989):
Redemption on a Farm

Not only is God present in the ordinary, but he is out to rescue us from ourselves. This is a central theme of *Cold Comfort Farm*,[12] a novel by English author Stella Gibbons, first published in 1932, then made into an outstanding film in 1996 by director John Schlesinger. Both the novel and the film tell a delightful story, a story about God's redemptive presence in ordinary human relationships and situations. *Cold Comfort Farm* is the kind of story that can't help but nourish a heart with no inclination to speak of God or Jesus in disrespectful ways.

Representing the redemptive Divine Mercy in *Cold Comfort Farm* is Flora Poste, age twenty. Flora has just completed an extensive formal education, her parents are recently deceased, and "she was discovered to possess every art and grace save that of earning her own living."[13]

With the help of her twenty-six-year-old wealthy widowed friend, Mrs. Smiling—eccentric in a sophisticated sort of way: her hobby is collecting "brassières"—Flora decides to stay with some distant relatives of her late father "in exchange for my beautiful eyes and a hundred pounds a year."

Flora goes to stay with the Starkadder family at their rural home, Cold Comfort Farm, where life is stuck in the mid-nineteenth century. Upon her arrival, Flora discovers that the farm is peopled with a variety of characters. Literally. Cold Comfort Farm itself represents the world at large, and its inhabitants are all of us. Flora's Aunt Judith Starkadder is a bitter, mysterious woman. Her two grown sons, Seth and Reuben, are unpredictable. Seth is a likable woman-chaser who dreams of becoming a movie star. Reuben's only happiness comes from working the farm, but he fears that Flora wants to claim ownership while he considers himself to be the rightful heir. Judith's husband, Amos, is in charge of the farm. He also marches off each Sunday to a nearby town to preach hellfire and brimstone in a peculiar little sectarian church.

But the most perplexing character of all is the grandmother, old Ada Starkadder, neé Doom, who never leaves her room on the second floor of the farmhouse but who has the entire farm and its dozen or so inhabitants completely under her control. For most of the novel—and the film—the only words Ada utters refer to some mysterious experience from her extremely distant childhood: "I saw something nasty in the woodshed!"

Flora Poste adapts herself to the personality of each person at Cold Comfort Farm, and gradually she helps each one find a kind of redemption, each in his or her own unique way. Seth leaves for Hollywood to be in the movies. Amos departs, cheered by his family, to preach in America. Reuben's dream to take over the farm is fulfilled. All are liberated from Ada's control to live their own lives. In spite of herself, Ada is freed from the awful task of keeping everyone under her thumb: off she goes to travel and see the world.

With the exception of its hilarious portrayal of Amos Starkadder's preaching, *Cold Comfort Farm* does not mention religion. Yet the novel is filled with a religious wisdom. The world of Cold Comfort Farm is a world where God is at work, a world where the Second Commandment makes every bit of sense imaginable because God is here and now. The final sentences celebrate the hope that is at the heart of any true religion, that gives life to anyone's prayer, that makes it absurd to even think of using sacred names in profane ways: "[Flora] glanced upwards for a second at the soft blue vault of the midsummer night sky. Not a cloud misted its solemn depths. Tomorrow would be a beautiful day."[14]

John Stewart (1939-):
Singing Our Way Home[15]

Popular music is a frantically mixed, frequently confusing business. There are musicians, however, whose work, while rarely generating the sales figures of the musical superstar, nevertheless reflects deep insights into the human experience of God in the midst of the ordinary. One such musician is John Stewart. His songs nourish a spirit that embraces the Second Commandment wholeheartedly.

John Stewart writes songs difficult to categorize. They are a mix of sometimes folk, sometimes rock, and a musical style that is uniquely John Stewart's own. Yet through much of his music, Stewart strings the results of his reflection on issues that are religious, issues that relate directly to the presence of the sacred in the ordinary. Sometimes John Stewart uses explicitly religious images—he is fond of angels as metaphors—but more often his songs address religious issues with little if any explicitly religious language. His songs are for the concert hall and the pub, not the church.

After seeing photographs of starving children in Africa, John Stewart wrote and recorded "Botswanna," a song that contrasts the dire poverty of these children with the empty affluence taken for granted by so many in the Western world:

> *Oh I live in California,*
> *I can look out at the ocean,*
> *On the silver blue Pacific,*
> *It is always there to see.*
> *But I'm so busy working*
> *That I don't have time to see it.*
> *But it's the knowing that it's there*
> *That means a lot to me.*

[Chorus:]

And it makes it hard
When I close my eyes,
When I can see the pictures
Taken at Botswanna
The pictures of the children
With flies in their eyes.

And those with all the money,
They are having nervous breakdowns,
And they're always taking pills
To make them feel the otherwise.
Oh how could I ever stumble
Or complain that things aren't
Going right,
How could I ever fail to see
Rainbows in the skies?

[Repeat Chorus]

Oh, faith it is a fire,
And it's fanned by the winds of thanks.
I am worried of our numbers,
And I'm worried of our ranks
As we fire up the Porsches,
Fighting to survive,
Then we look for valet parking
Out on Rodeo Drive.

[Repeat Chorus]

And it makes it hard:
I wonder if God cries
When He sees the pictures
That were taken at Botswanna,
The pictures of the children
With the flies in their eyes.

And I'm not my brother's keeper
For I do not have the power,
As if part of some great game
They play on the other side.
Because it's all that I can do
To just keep myself together.
Still I see faces in the
        Blue Pacific tide.

[Repeat Chorus]

Is it not for us to wonder,
Is it not for us to cry out?
For we are but a family without walls,
But we have waters.
And every face you see is you
And it is I....

[Repeat Chorus][16]

As John Stewart sings this song from beginning to end, the voice of a female backup singer chants over and over the Latin phrase *"Credo Domino"* ("I believe, Lord"). This changes the song from being merely a song about compassion for suffering children to an expression of compassion couched in a moving statement of religious belief. "Botswanna" is a song about children who are suffering. It is about empty affluence, spiritual emptiness, drug abuse, and about the unity of all humankind. It is also an expression of helplessness. All of these are presented in the context of faith in God and, by implication, as a petition for divine assistance. To listen to this song is to come face to face with the sacred in the ordinary, and the listener is left with a greater sensitivity to God's presence, a stronger inclination to live in the spirit of the Second Commandment.

Another John Stewart song deals with the need for personal and spiritual transformation. "Ghost Inside of Me" begins "Every prayer I could be praying, / Every promise I am betraying, / Every price that I am paying / is like a ghost inside of me." The song continues, listing various ways we fail to be all that we could be: "Every road I could be taking, / Every dream I am forsaking / is like a ghost inside of me."[17]

This song is rooted in a deep perception of human failings and limitations. It is a musical admission of the need to be changed from the inside out, and as such it is a poignant expression of the sacred in the ordinary and of the human need for God. "So look around, 'round look around / Every time I turn around / I'm not who I ought to be."

Many of John Stewart's songs are loaded with words and images to spark a renewed sensitivity to the sacred in the secular, a new appreciation for the spirit of the Second Commandment. His songs carry words and images to open the heart to God in the most ordinary situations. For John Stewart, there is no getting lost in life because as one of his songs reminds us, no matter where we go, "an angel on the road shoulder knows the way home."[18]

Nancy Willard (1936-):
Intersecting Eternity With the Ordinary

Finally, we turn to the work of novelist, poet, and children's author Nancy Willard. Two of her novels—*Things Invisible to See* and *Sister Water*—are sacred stories about the most ordinary people in the most ordinary situations, about people who have the most remarkable lives and whose experiences open up for readers the sacred dimension of their own everyday existence. Willard's fiction nourishes sensitivity to the holy in the ordinary, where the spirit of the Second Commandment can thrive.

From the first words of *Things Invisible to See*, the reader knows that this will not be an ordinary novel:

> In Paradise, on the banks of the River of Time, the Lord of the Universe is playing ball with His archangels. Hundred of spheres rest like white stones on the bottom of the river, and hundreds rise like bubbles from the water and fly to His hand that alone brings things to pass and gives them their true colors. What a show! He tosses a white ball which breaks into a yellow ball which breaks into a red ball, and in the northeast corner of the Sahara Desert the sand shifts and buries eight camels. The two herdsmen escape, and in a small town in southern Michigan Wanda Harkissian goes into labor with twins. She will name them Ben and Willie, but it's Esau and Jacob all over again.[19]

From there on, *Things Invisible to See*—the title is from seventeenth-century English poet John Donne—is the story of ordinary people's lives intersecting with eternity, of baseball and angels, good people and evil demons. It's a story of love and life beyond life. On every page, Nancy Willard brings us face to face with the sacred that is present in the everyday, with a world where the Second Commandment is taken for granted.

Another Nancy Willard novel, *Sister Water*, is a twist on the old adage that when God closes a door, he opens a window. It's a story about human love as a carrier of divine love: about a man and a woman, about good and evil, about life and death, and about an angel. In the closing scene Jessie, the main character, is dying:

> The angel at the foot of her bed was as magnificent as he had been at her first sight of him when she lay hidden in the cellar of the house where she was born. His hawk's head did not frighten her; she knew it was his true face….
>
> "I leave to children exclusively," whispered the angel in a voice of infinite sweetness, "but only for the life of their childhood, the dandelions of the field and the daisies thereof, with the right to play among them freely, according to the custom of children, warning them at the same time against the thistles."
>
> "Why, I know those words!" exclaimed Jessie.
>
> "Appropriate, don't you think?" murmured the angel. "We try to make the departures a little special." He offered her his shining sleeve, and, leaving her old body to fend for itself, she accepted. At the bend in the river she heard the heavenly choir singing, "Just As the Tide Was Flowing." Leaves, roots, Niagara Falls on porcelain, Sam's shoes in the cellar, The Everpresent Fullness [her cat] purring at the foot of her bed—everything was letting her go….

"My daughter Ellen—I want you to give her a gift."
"What gift?" asked the angel.
"Wings."[20]

Among Nancy Willard's other books, *A Visit to William Blake's Inn* is ostensibly for children.[21] In truth, however, it is a book filled with the spirit of childhood, a spirit to which adults are wise to aspire, a spirit that wouldn't think of acting contrary to the Second Commandment. It is a beautifully illustrated volume that stands as a literary metaphor for the ability to see that the secret in the sacred is not somber but delightful. The book is a loosely connected series of poems. The first one begins

> *This inn belongs to William Blake*
> *and many are the beasts he's tamed*
> *and many are the stars he's named*
> *and many those who stop and take*
> *their joyful rest with William Blake.*
>
> *Two mighty dragons brew and bake*
> *and many are the loaves they've burned*
> *and many are the spits they've turned*
> *and many those who stop and break*
> *their joyful bread with William Blake.*[22]

The poems recount marvelous adventures and unspeakable joys, and in the end, without the poems ever saying so explicitly, the reader is left with a deep sense that just out of reach, but closer to us than we are ourselves, there is an Absolute Delight that wants nothing more than to fill the human heart. Again, from this perception you couldn't imagine ever speaking of this Absolute Delight in any but the most grateful and respectful terms.

On its final page, Nancy Willard's collection of playful poems comes as close as it ever does to making this point, but it is all between the lines.

> *My adventures now are ended.*
> *I and all whom I befriended*
> *from this holy hill I must go*
> *home to lives we left below.*
>
> *Farewell cow and farewell cat,*
> *rabbit, tiger, sullen rat.*
> *To our children we shall say*
> *how we walked the Milky Way.*
>
> *You whose journeys now begin,*
> *if you reach a lovely inn,*
> *if a rabbit makes your bed,*
> *if two dragons bake your bread,*
> *rest a little for my sake,*
> *and give my love to William Blake.*[23]

Along with Stevie Smith, John Stewart, Stella Gibbons, Shusaku Endo, and Vincent Van Gogh, Nancy Willard urges us to overcome the Western dichotomy between the sacred and the secular by showing us the holiness of everyday things. With her stories and poems she leaves us holding a gift, and the gift is God's presence in the ordinary, a natural consequence when we observe the Second Commandment.

Notes

1. Richard J. Clifford, S.J., "Exodus," in Raymond E. Brown, S.S., et al., editors, *The New Jerome Biblical Commentary* (Englewood Cliffs, NJ: Prentice Hall, 1990), 52.

2. Craig M. Gay, *The Way of the (Modern) World: Or, Why It's Tempting to Live As If God Doesn't Exist* (Grand Rapids, MI: Wm. B. Eerdmans Publishing Company, 1998), 2.

3. Sheila Cassidy, interviewed for "Monasticism as Rebellion." The Canadian Broadcasting Corporation, 1986.

4. *New Selected Poems of Stevie Smith* (New York: New Directions Publishing Corp., 1988), 93.

5. Stevie Smith, 2.

6. Stevie Smith, 3.

7. Cliff Edwards, *Van Gogh and God: A Creative Spiritual Quest* (Chicago: Loyola Press, 1989), 142.

8. Quoted by Edwards, 142.

9. Quoted by Edwards, 79.

10. Shusaku Endo, *Wonderful Fool*, translated by Francis Mathy (New York: Harper & Row, 1988).

11. Endo, 237.

12. Stella Gibbons, *Cold Comfort Farm* (New York: Penguin Books, 1977, 1996).

13. Gibbons, 11.

14. Gibbons, 233.

15. For a catalog of John Stewart's recordings, write: Homecoming Records, P.O. Box 2050, Malibu, CA 90265–7050. Phone: (818) 345–6579. E-mail: HcomingRec@aol.com.

16. John Stewart, "Botswanna" (Bugle Music, BMI), included on compact disk *Punch the Big Guy*. Schanachie Entertainment Corp., CD No. 8009. Reprinted with permission of John Stewart.

17. John Stewart, "Ghost Inside of Me" (Bugle/Bug Publishing). Included on *Escape to Arizona*. Audiocassette, Homecoming Records.

18. John Stewart, "Angel on the Road Shoulder." Included on compact disk *Chilly Winds*. Homecoming Records/Folk Era Productions, 1993.

19. Nancy Willard, *Things Invisible to See* (New York: Alfred A. Knopf, 1984), 3.

20. Nancy Willard, *Sister Water* (New York: Ballantine/Ivy Books, 1993), 245–247.

21. *A Visit to William Blake's Inn: Poems for Innocent and Experienced Travelers*, by Nancy Willard. Illustrated by Alice and Martin Provensen (New York: Harcourt, Brace & Co., 1981).

22. Nancy Willard, Ibid., 14.

23. Nancy Willard, Ibid., 44.

Chapter 4

THE THIRD
COMMANDMENT

Catechetical Formula

Remember to keep holy the LORD'S Day.

Scriptural Version

Remember the sabbath day, and keep it holy. Six days you shall labor and do all your work. But the seventh day is a sabbath to the LORD your God; you shall not do any work—you, your son or your daughter, your male or female slave, your livestock, or the alien resident in your towns. For in six days the LORD made heaven and earth, the sea, and all that is in them, but rested the seventh day; therefore the LORD blessed the sabbath day and consecrated it.

EXODUS 20:8–11

P ope John Paul II called the Jewish people our elder brothers and sisters, and if ever we could learn something from our elder siblings in faith it would be about how to observe the Third Commandment. Most Catholics, if they do anything to "keep holy the LORD's Day," figure their duty is done if they "go to Mass."

If you want to start a cultural revolution, try to get great numbers of people to take seriously the Third Commandment. Of course, in the present cultural climate this idea has a snowball's chance in July. So completely secularized is our culture, so dominant is the business ethos, so powerful is the belief that work and buying and selling can and should happen at any time of the day or night, 7 days a week, 365 days a year, that most people view with distrust any suggestion that we should stop doing these things one day a week.

You want to go to church on Sunday? Fine, that's your private concern. But be sure to mow your lawn and go shopping and work if your employer or your business requires it.

The Jewish perspective on the Sabbath is different. Of course, for Judaism the Sabbath is from sundown Friday until sundown on Saturday. Since the end of the first century, Christianity—with the exception of late-blooming (nineteenth-century) groups such as the Seventh-Day Adventists—has observed the Sabbath on Sunday, in commemoration of the Resurrection of Christ, which happened on a Sunday.[1] All the same, the principle is identical, namely, the need to observe the Sabbath as a holy day.

THE JEWISH SENSE OF SABBATH

Before we discuss what "keeping holy the LORD's Day" might mean for Catholics today, considerable light may be shed on the discussion if we take a look at how contemporary Judaism understands the Sabbath observance.

For Orthodox Jews, the Sabbath, or *Shabbat*, is a weekly religious festival. According to the Torah—the Scriptures and oral traditions of Judaism—the Sabbath celebrates two events: the creation of the world by God and the liberation of Israel from slavery in Egypt.

Why remember and celebrate these two events weekly? In the first instance, the creation, the purpose is to remind humans that they are called to be Godlike. According to the Book of Genesis, "God rested (2:3) on the seventh day of creation. For Jews, then, Shabbat exists "to teach us that just as God stopped creating physical things on the seventh day, so man is to stop creating on this day. Man is to stop making things, to stop manipulating nature. He is to let all things run by themselves. By desisting from all such labors, we not only acknowledge the existence of a Creator, but also emulate the Divine example."[2]

The second Sabbath theme is the liberation of Israel from slavery in Egypt. Again, why remember and celebrate this event weekly? The idea is for Jews to remember their slavery in the past in order to cherish their freedom in the present. "If the Sabbath on the one hand emphasizes our servitude to God, it also stresses our *freedom from servitude to human masters*. It emphasizes the freedom of the human soul, the freedom of mind and body.

> From sunset on Friday to sunset on the Saturday no work nor travel is permitted. Candles are lit to commemorate the light of God, the light of the world and the light of the faith, and also because in an Orthodox house, no one may switch on a lamp or light a fire. The Shabbat is, as well as a time for prayer and remembrance, also a time for eating and drinking and being jolly.[3]

The most important Sabbath ritual takes place not in the synagogue but in the home. The household gathers around the table to celebrate the beginning of Shabbat with the lighting of candles, prayers, and blessings. If you have seen a stage production or the movie version of *Fiddler on the Roof*, you have some idea of how a Jewish Sabbath begins on Friday evening.

Novelist Herman Wouk describes wonderfully the mood of a modern Sabbath in a Jewish home:

> The pious Jew on the Sabbath does not travel, or cook, or use motors or electric appliances, or spend money, or smoke, or write. The industrial world stops dead for him. Nearly all the mechanical advantages of civilization drop away. The voice of the radio is still; the television screen is blank. The movies, the baseball and football games, the golf courses, the theatres, the night clubs, the highways, the card tables, the barbeque pits—indeed most of the things that make up the busy pleasures of conventional leisure—are not for him. The Jewish Sabbath is a ceremony that makes steep demands to achieve a decisive effect. A Jew who undertakes to observe it is, from sundown Friday, to the end of twilight on Saturday, in a world cut off.[4]

This may sound like a grim existence, but that attitude only shows how completely enculturated we are, how dependent we are on the whiz-bangs of a technological society. We think our televisions and VCRs and stereo systems and computers and cars and microwave ovens are necessary for even a modicum of happiness. In fact, the Third Commandment leads us to wonder whether we own our technology or our technology owns us.

Note that the ancient Israelites did not have names for the days of the week except for the last day, the Sabbath (Hebrew _abb_t). All the other days were merely numbered. The word *sabbath* is related to the verb _bt, which means "coming/bringing to an end."[5] This, of course, is what happens on the Sabbath, an end to work, a time of rest and leisure in the truest sense of the word.

Among the ancient Israelites, strict regulations developed to protect the Sabbath observance and make it absolute. In the Gospels we find some evidence for the debates that developed in rabbinic Judaism over Sabbath observance.[6] Eventually, a regulation emerged to govern exceptions to Sabbath limitations: "Every case of danger of life allows for the suspension of the Sabbath."[7]

Later, other rabbinic authorities taught that "one should not desecrate the Sabbath for things that can be done the day before or the day after, but no desecration exists when such a possibility is not offered."[8] Thus, for example, a midwife may deliver a baby on the Sabbath, and she may receive help from others.

As mentioned above, the Gospels reflect a conflict between Jesus and rabbinic Judaism concerning Sabbath observance. Jesus opposed a legalistic observance that would make human needs subservient to legalisms. One of the best known and most typical examples is in the Gospel of Luke:

> He was teaching in a synagogue on the sabbath. And just then there appeared a woman with a spirit that had crippled her for eighteen years. She was bent over and was quite unable to stand up straight. When Jesus saw her, he called her over and said, "Woman, you are set free from your ailment." When he laid his hands on her, immediately she stood up straight and began praising God. But the leader of the syna-

gogue, indignant because Jesus had cured on the sabbath, kept saying to the crowd, "There are six days on which work ought to be done; come on those days and be cured, and not on the sabbath day." But the Lord answered him and said, "You hypocrites! Does not each of you on the sabbath untie his ox or his donkey from the manger, and lead it away to give it water? And ought not this woman, a daughter of Abraham, whom Satan bound for eighteen long years, be set free from this bondage on the sabbath day?" When he said this, all his opponents were put to shame; and the entire crowd was rejoicing at all the wonderful things that he was doing (Lk 13:10–17).

The difference between the perspective of Jesus and that of the "leader of the synagogue" is one of priorities. For Jesus, the Sabbath exists for a higher purpose, and that higher purpose may sometimes nullify the rules for Sabbath observance. The spirit and reality of the Sabbath are "bigger" than Sabbath rules and regulations. For the "leader of the synagogue," on the contrary, the Sabbath cannot be separated from the rules for its observance. For Jesus, the Sabbath and its rules are relative; for the "leader of the synagogue" the two are one, so the rules are absolutes, ends in themselves. Jesus states his position best himself when he declares in the Gospel of Mark, "The sabbath was made for humankind, and not humankind for the sabbath; so the Son of Man is lord even of the sabbath" (2:27–28).

Modern Jewish observance of the Sabbath still takes Sabbath rules seriously as indispensable guides that are necessary to the preservation of the true spirit of the Sabbath. Lest we think of the modern Jewish Sabbath as a grim business, however, Herman Wouk reassures us that just the opposite is true:

...this day is the fulcrum of a practicing Jew's existence and generally a source of strength, refreshment, and cheer....Our Sabbath opens with blessings over light and wine. Light and wine are the keys to the day. Our observance has its solemnities, but the main effect is release, peace, gaiety, and lifted spirits.[9]

Is there a need and a place for the Sabbath in our time? Rabbi Hayim Halevy Donin thinks so:

Modern man may celebrate many holidays, but he observes few holy days. He may possess many more hours and days of leisure than those in previous generations, but he still lacks days of serenity and tranquility.[10]

Perhaps the greatest modern Jewish commentator on the Sabbath was Abraham Joshua Heschel (1907–1972). In his foundational book, *The Sabbath*, Heschel articulated a love for and an understanding of the Sabbath observance that is unsurpassed.[11] Heschel organized his book into three parts, each of which takes a unique approach to discussing the Sabbath as the sanctification of time.

What does the word "Sabbath" mean? According to some it is the name of the Holy One. Since the word Shabbat is a name of God, one should not mention it in unclean places, where words of Torah should not be spoken. Some people were careful not to take it in vain.

The seventh day is like a palace in time with a kingdom for all. It is not a date but an atmosphere.

It is not a different state of consciousness but a

different climate; it is as if the appearance of all things somehow changed. The primary awareness is one of our being within the Sabbath rather than of the Sabbath being within us. We may not know whether our understanding is correct, or whether our sentiments are noble, but the air of the day surrounds us like spring which spreads over the land without our aid or notice.[12]

For Heschel, Judaism is a religion not of space but of time. Judaism finds meaning not in space and the things people make to fill space, but in time and the eternal that penetrates time. "On the Sabbath it is given us to share in the holiness that is in the heart of time."[13]

SUNDAY IN A CATHOLIC CONTEXT

As we have already noted, the early Christians continued the Sabbath observance but soon moved the Sabbath to the first day of the week, Sunday, because the Resurrection of Jesus happened on a Sunday. "From the fourth century on, councils and Christian legislation frequently mandated cessation from work and attendance at worship on Sunday."[14]

Jumping back to a Catholic context, there is no shortage of evidence that official Church teachings and legislation continue to support this understanding of Sunday as a day for worship and rest. The *Catechism of the Catholic Church* (n. 2192–2193) quotes the Code of Canon Law:

"Sunday...is to be observed as the foremost holy day of obligation in the universal Church" (can. 1246). "On Sundays and other holy days of obligation the faithful are bound to participate in the Mass" (can. 1247). "On Sundays and other holy days of obligation the faithful are bound...to abstain from those labors and business concerns which impede the worship to be rendered to God, the joy which is proper to the Lord's Day, or the proper relaxation of mind and body" (can. 1247).

All such official teachings notwithstanding, you don't need a Ph.D. in cultural anthropology to see that in the overwhelming majority of Catholic lives there is little difference between how we spend the Lord's Day and how we live the other days of the week. If we are fortunate, we do not have to work on Sundays, but many Catholics have little or no choice about this if they want to keep their jobs. For many Catholic workers, their days off may be Tuesday and Wednesday, or some other days, instead of the traditional Saturday and Sunday. We no longer inhabit a culture with a shared sense of time, with sacred times set aside for sacred purposes. Rather, all time is secular; all time is a virtual commodity to be consumed, used up, and that's the end of that. How can we make room for the spirit of the Sabbath in such cultural circumstances?

For a great many Catholics, only Sunday Mass attendance—and sometimes this occurs on Saturday evening—marks a difference between them and people for whom Sunday is just another day. Indeed, recent surveys suggest that a great many Catholics don't even attend Mass every Sunday. So enculturated are most Catholics—so steeped are we in the popular culture of our time and place—that apart from Sunday Mass we use Sundays in the same ways everyone else uses Sundays, and observing all of Sunday as the Lord's Day is not high on the list of priorities for most Catholics.

Devout Jews have a Sabbath tradition that supports a countercultural Sabbath observance. This is one of the main practices that makes Jews unique, that sets them apart, and they can be grateful for this. Among devout Jews there is considerable communal support for the kind of Sabbath observance Herman Wouk and Rabbi Heschel describe. Among Catholics there is no such tradition and no longer such communal support.

A few generations ago, there may have been more of a shared sense among Catholics, and other Christians, too, that Sunday was "a day of rest." Many stores and businesses remained closed on Sunday. But today these "day-of-rest" social and cultural conditions are a thing of the past. Any Catholic family, or any individual Catholic, wanting to take to heart and live out a true observance of Sunday as the Lord's Day swims upstream against a strong current.

Ironically, widespread Catholic indifference to a serious observance of the Lord's Day is the result, in part at least, of a praiseworthy strand of Catholic tradition. Catholicism looks for and finds the sacred in the secular, the holy in the ordinary. Catholicism wants nothing to do with theological dualism. But because it is so open to the holy in the everyday, Catholicism is also inclined to lose sight of the need sometimes to set aside times and places as holy in special ways. This is one reason the Lord's Day observance has virtually vanished among Catholics in the so-called developed countries.

If the Catholic community could generate widespread interest in a countercultural observance of the Lord's Day, this would result in nothing short of a major social and cultural shift, given the numbers of Catholics in the world. The more Catholics willing to make the sacrifices needed for such an observance, the more likely this transformation will become. Nothing short of a major evangelization effort followed by a generous, openhearted response is likely to make this happen, however.

A SACRED SENSE OF LEISURE

Part of such an evangelization effort would need to include a philosophical and theological rationale for observing Sunday as a day of prayer and leisure. One of the great classics of our time that may provide at least a starting point for developing such a rationale was first published in English in 1952. German Catholic philosopher Josef Pieper wrote *Leisure: The Basis of Culture* to explain what leisure is and why it is so important to the quality of human existence and human culture.[15]

Josef Pieper suggests that leisure is an attitude of mind and a condition of the soul that fosters a capacity to perceive reality as it is. In order to have genuine leisure, of course, there must be time(s) set aside when nothing happens of any significance to the world of commerce. Not so remarkably, such a time would look for Christians much like the Jewish Sabbath described by Herman Wouk and celebrated by Abraham Heschel. It would be a day of worship with a local faith community, then it would be a day of quiet, rest, reading, and more quiet—in short, a day of authentic leisure.

Josef Pieper's book was published in German in 1947, so that long ago he sounded a clarion call for a return to authentic leisure. Unless we regain the art of silence and a thirst for insight, an ability to be inactive, he said; unless we begin to put genuine leisure in the place of frantic forms of amusement, we will destroy ourselves and our world. There is, in fact, in the human heart a craving for the Sabbath, and that may be one of our few opportunities for a salvation that has any meaning in this world.

Can Christians recover an authentic experience of the Lord's Day? Speaking from a Catholic perspective, it seems evident that Catholicism, at least, treasures the seeds of the

Lord's Day. The opportunity and the resources are there. It's only a question of whether or not Catholics will use them.

Josef Pieper's point is that authentic leisure—we may say the leisure that characterizes the true spirit of Sabbath and the Lord's Day—is absolutely necessary if a culture is to keep in touch with all that is most deeply human and is to survive. All we need do is look around at the dominant popular culture of our own time, at how superficial, inane, and frequently violent much of it is, to see the truth of Pieper's insight. The dominant popular culture is humanly and spiritually bankrupt because we rarely, if ever, experience authentic leisure. And this is so, Pieper says, because true leisure "is not possible unless it has a durable and consequently living link with the *cultus*, with divine worship."[16]

In other words, the dominant popular culture is largely crazy because we have lost touch with the experience of divine worship offered by an authentic, lived religion. Many people substitute either religious indifference or religious tokenism. Many others cultivate a religion or "spirituality" that welcomes with open arms a radical dichotomy between sacred and secular and so has little if any impact on the dominant culture which goes its mindless way completely out of touch with the leisure that only divine worship can make possible.

Josef Pieper wrote that divine worship is the only source of true human "freedom, independence, and immunity within society."[17] This is why the dominant popular culture is so unhealthy and such a threat to all that is most deeply human. Apart from regular experiences of Sabbath/Lord's Day leisure, our immunity to all that is most dehumanizing in the popular culture is greatly reduced.

That said, it is also true that at its most basic the leisure that characterizes the true spirit of Sabbath does not depend on a strict observance of Sabbath, per se. Rather, what matters is an *attitude* that we can cultivate at all times. Pieper wrote:

> Leisure, it must be clearly understood, is a mental and spiritual attitude—it is not simply the result of spare time, a holiday, a weekend or a vacation. It is, in the first place, an attitude of mind, a condition of the soul, and as such utterly contrary to the ideal of "worker"....
>
> Compared with the exclusive ideal of work as activity, leisure implies (in the first place) an attitude of nonactivity, of inward calm, of silence; it means not being "busy," but letting things happen.
>
> Leisure is a form of silence, of that silence which is the prerequisite of the apprehension of reality; only the silent hear and those who do not remain silent do not hear....
>
> Furthermore, there is also a certain serenity in leisure....[18]

The spirit of Sabbath, and the spirit of the Lord's Day, is one that a traditional observance of Sabbath/Lord's Day helps us to cultivate. In a culture that has lost touch with the need for special times set aside as sacred, however, we need not lose touch entirely with the experience of sacred leisure and the freedom sacred leisure gives.

Loss of the Lord's Day is one of the negative consequences of Catholicism's conviction that the holy can be discovered in the ordinary, which includes the dominant popular culture. Let an official Church teaching declare that on Sundays there should be no television, no out-of-the-home recreational activities, that Sundays must be days that look much like a traditional Jewish Sabbath, and there will be a second rejection of an official Church teaching by the vast majority of Catholics.[19]

Catholics are too deeply embedded in their culture to embrace a Lord's Day observance of leisure, worship, prayer, and quiet family activities in the home. Still, the spirit of Sabbath and the spirit of the Lord's Day—the spirit of leisure as Josef Pieper understood it—can and should be a part of what it means to be Catholic. If we can't hope to have Sundays become a major countercultural experience at least we can take advantage of other traditional ways to encourage the spirit of sacred leisure.

Participation in Sunday Mass remains fundamental, of course. But there are several other traditional ways to cultivate the sacred in the ordinary. Catholics can make time in every day for a moment of quiet prayerfulness. We can take steps to make our homes quieter places to live in and be with others. We can place limits on television watching. We can encourage reading. We can take advantage of opportunities to go on retreats and days of recollection. Also, there seems to be a resurgence of interest among Catholics in eucharistic devotions, including adoration of the Blessed Sacrament. This is a beneficial development as long as eucharistic devotions are theologically balanced and healthy, and as long as such devotions are not tied to various religious ideologies.

The gospel liberates us from legalistic observances of all kinds. But the spirit of the Sabbath/Lord's Day is essential to a full, adult Christian life. It is up to us to live that spirit in a popular culture that offers little support for such a concern. When we do this, the positive impact on heart, mind, and spirit will be incalculable, not to mention the positive impact on the faith community at large.

Notes

1. See J. A. Soggin, "Sabbath," in Bruce M. Metzger and Michael D. Coogan, eds., *The Oxford Companion to the Bible* (New York: Oxford University Press, 1993), 665.

2. Rabbi Hayim Halevy Donin, *To Be a Jew: A Guide to Jewish Observance in Contemporary Life* (New York: Basic Books, 1972, 1991), 65.

3. Liz Flower, *The Elements of World Religions* (Rockport, MA: Element Books, 1997), 13.

4. Herman Wouk, *This Is My God: The Jewish Way of Life*, Revised Edition (New York: Pocket Books, 1974), 38.

5. Soggin, 665.

6. See, for example, Matthew 12:1–14 and Mark 3:1–6.

7. Soggin, 665.

8. Soggin, 665.

9. Wouk, 38.

10. Donin, 70.

11. Abraham Joshua Heschel, *The Sabbath* (New York: Farrar, Straus, Giroux, 1951).

12. Heschel, 20–21.

13. Heschel, 101.

14. Richard P. McBrien, General Ed., *The HarperCollins Encyclopedia of Catholicism* (San Francisco: HarperSanFrancisco, 1995), 1146.

15. Josef Pieper, *Leisure: The Basis of Culture* (New York: Mentor Books/New American Classics, 1952, 1963).

16. Pieper, 17.

17. Pieper, 17.

18. Pieper, 40–41.

19. The first was, of course, the prohibition of artificial contraceptives by Pope Paul VI in his 1968 encyclical, *Humanae Vitae*.

Chapter 5

THE FOURTH COMMANDMENT

Catechetical Formula

> Honor your father and your mother.

Scriptural Version

> Honor your father and your mother, so that your days may be long in the land that the LORD your God is giving you.
>
> EXODUS 20:12

In 1999 the state of Louisiana passed a law requiring children in public schools to address teachers as "ma'am" or "sir." That means a teacher may reprimand a child, send the child to the principal's office, or call the child's parents for a failure to say, "Yes, sir" or "No, sir," "Yes, ma'am" or "No, ma'am" in reply to a question from a teacher or other adult. This law was enacted because of concern that children were not consistently showing respect for their teachers and other adults.

Is this yet another example of a culture gone amuck, a society that has forgotten the Ten Commandments—in this case, the Fourth Commandment? Perhaps. But maybe the reason for disrespect on the part of children for adult authority figures is more complex than that.

SCRIPTURAL ROOTS OF THE FOURTH COMMANDMENT

First, let's take a look at the biblical roots of the Fourth Commandment. The first three commandments address our relationship with God. With the Fourth Commandment the focus shifts to our relationships with one another. "God has willed that, after him, we should honor our parents to whom we owe life and who have handed on to us the knowledge of God."[1]

Scripturally, the Fourth Commandment is unique because it has some intriguing New Testament echoes. Also, it is the first commandment to state a consequence for its observance. Of course, in our time, the Fourth Commandment opens up the can of psychological, emotional, sociological, and even ecclesiological worms called parent/child relationships. Whether you took Psychology 101 or not, we inherit from the dominant culture a belief in the conviction that children are indelibly marked by their relationship with their parents, for good and for ill. Considerable blaming goes on as a result, but that's another topic.

In ancient Israelite culture, an oral society, parents were synonymous with "elders." They carried the traditions of the culture. As they grew older, parents also depended on their grown offspring to care for them. The instances in the

Gospels where Jesus interacts with Mary and—in one case—Joseph suggest some intriguing Christian perspectives on the Fourth Commandment.

The only narrative we have from the childhood of Jesus is, of course, the story in Luke's Gospel where the twelve-year-old Jesus is accidentally left behind in Jerusalem and found, four days later, in the Temple. We find the key interaction in this narrative in its concluding lines:

> When his parents saw him they were astonished; and his mother said to him, "Child, why have you treated us like this? Look, your father and I have been searching for you in great anxiety." He said to them, "Why were you searching for me? Did you not know that I must be in my Father's house?" But they did not understand what he said to them. Then he went down with them and came to Nazareth, and was obedient to them (Lk 2:48–51).

As far as the Gospel of Luke is concerned, Jesus' relationship with his Father takes priority over his relationship with his earthly parents. In this narrative, there is clearly something bigger going on in Jesus' life than Mary and Joseph are capable of understanding. At the same time Luke, and Jesus, honor the Fourth Commandment. The boy Jesus does not insist on remaining in Jerusalem; he returns to Nazareth and is "obedient" to Mary and Joseph.

Even earlier than the Gospel of Luke, of course, are the Pauline letters. The Letter to the Ephesians comments upon and quotes the version of the Fourth Commandment in Deuteronomy 5:16:

Children, obey your parents in the Lord, for this is
right. "Honor your father and mother"—this is the
First Commandment with a promise: "so that it may
be well with you and you may live long on the earth"
(Eph 6:1–3).

Notice, however, that the author—probably not Paul
himself[2]—immediately adds a corresponding "commandment" meant for parents:

And, fathers, do not provoke your children to anger,
but bring them up in the discipline and instruction
of the Lord (Eph 6:4).

With this sentence, the New Testament adds a recipro-
cal perspective not found in the Hebrew Scriptures. It's as if
the author of Ephesians was saying that parents can't simply quote the Fourth Commandment to their children, for
children have human dignity that deserves respect, too. At
the same time, parents have an obligation to instruct and
train their children in the Christian life. Since the Fourth
Commandment remains in effect, of course, children have
an obligation to honor and respect their parents.

The author of the Letter to the Ephesians says, in effect,
that children and parents need to respect one another, and
both parents and children have their proper place in the
relationship. For Ephesians, we are not talking about complete egalitarianism or even democracy. Rather, parents and
children have their proper roles, and children are not equal
to adults.

This leaves a great deal of room for modern psycholo-
gists, experts on parenting, and authorities on caring for
your elderly parents. None of these need ever worry that
either the Fourth Commandment or the Letter to the

Ephesians will put them out of business. We can, and should, ponder the Fourth Commandment and its discussion in the Letter to the Ephesians. But in the end modern parents—and their offspring—are left with big questions about how to interpret this commandment in our own time and place.

HONORING PARENTS IN TODAY'S WORLD

Essentially, the Fourth Commandment and its addendum from the Letter to the Ephesians are about family life, for parent-child relationships are what constitute family life in the traditional sense. Of course, parent-child relationships go beyond the child-rearing years to the decades when parent and grown offspring relate to each other as adult-to-adult. The Fourth Commandment covers the entire spectrum of parent-offspring relationships, from the adult-infant years to the aged parent-adult offspring years. Indeed, the Fourth Commandment takes all this for granted, and what it doesn't explicitly cover is covered by its addendum in the Letter to the Ephesians.

The Fourth Commandment takes for granted that the "child" who hears is at least old enough to reason and act in a relatively mature, responsible, moral fashion. For all practical purposes, we must admit that the Fourth Commandment is addressed to older adolescents and adults whose parents are still living. In ancient Israel, of course, people rarely lived longer than their mid forties to early fifties. Someone who lived into the sixth or seventh decade was considered ancient, indeed.

But the point is that the Fourth Commandment tells young adults and adult "children" to "honor" their parents. It is highly significant that the Fourth Commandment names both father and mother, thus indicating a greater degree of equality than we would expect in this ancient culture. "The law condemned the faults of children against their mother as much as offenses against their father...," wrote Old Testament scholar Father Roland de Vaux, O.P.[3] Here are three examples:

> You shall each revere your mother and father... (Lev 19:3).

> All who curse father or mother shall be put to death; having cursed father or mother, their blood is upon them (Lev 20:9).

> If someone has a stubborn and rebellious son who will not obey his father and mother, who does not heed them when they discipline him, then his father and his mother shall take hold of him and bring him out to the elders of his town at the gate of that place. They shall say to the elders of his town, "This son of ours is stubborn and rebellious. He will not obey us. He is a glutton and a drunkard." Then all the men of the town shall stone him to death (Deut 21:18–21a).

When it came to unmanageable adolescents, there was no "tough love" for the ancient Israelites! It was shape up or kiss yourself goodbye! The point, of course, is that child, adolescent, and adult offspring were expected to honor, respect, and obey their parents. The ancient Israelites were innocent of modern psychology, and while we may be tempted to envy them for this, we do not live in ancient Israel. We can only live in our own time and place, and we need to interpret and apply the Fourth Commandment here and now.

What, then, does it mean to "honor your father and

your mother" in the twenty-first century, in a pluralistic Western culture, where theories about parent-child relationships are not in short supply? Truth to tell, it may not be as complicated or difficult to understand as we may suspect. There are always instances where adolescents and adults fail to respect their parents, where verbal and even physical abuse takes place. But in the overwhelming majority of situations adults know, intuitively, what it means to love, honor, and respect parents.

Today, we tend to interpret ordinary adolescent disrespect for parents as a manifestation of immaturity more than anything else. The basic issue is how adolescents can learn to express negative feelings in respectful ways. Modern parenting theories agree that adolescents need to learn respectful behavior toward parents and other people in general.[4]

HONORING OUR ELDERS

More to the point when it comes to a modern interpretation and application of the Fourth Commandment, however, is appropriate actions on the part of adults toward their aging or elderly parents. This is not only appropriate today, it is closer to the original purpose of the Fourth Commandment.

Today, the Fourth Commandment leads to a plethora of practical issues. With modern health care, people live longer on the average today than they ever did before. This means that adult offspring frequently find themselves dealing simultaneously with an "empty nest," their own children recently grown and gone, and the needs of aging parents. Just when they begin to feel free of the obligations of child rearing, they begin to feel fettered by the need to care for elderly parents. What, then, does the Fourth Commandment mean for this "sandwich generation"?

It helps little to simply declare the need to "honor your father and your mother." The question, in practical everyday terms, is *how* are we to "honor" our aging parents when their needs seem so complicated to deal with? It's not as if all we need do is make a few simple choices then carry them out. Instead, many complex social, economic, emotional, and medical issues flock to the scene the minute we try to deal with these choices.[5]

Given all this, it may come as a surprise that the Fourth Commandment, after all, hits the nail on the head. Regardless of the issue at hand, we are obliged to honor and respect our aging parents; indeed, they have a *right* to our honor and respect.[6]

Take one of the most common situations, when it becomes evident that aging parents can no longer live a completely independent life in their own home. To "honor" the parent means not making a unilateral decision that you then impose with an announcement that this is the way it's going to be. Instead, you respect the parent's feelings, you talk about it, you listen to the parent's concerns and fears, and you help him or her to participate in the decision-making process, as long as the parent is mentally and emotionally competent to do so. Even in cases where the parent is no longer able to participate in making decisions and choices, he or she deserves kindness, care, and respect. In other words, the parent has a right to be *included*.

Sometimes older people go to great lengths to retain as much control over their lives as possible. A novel full of insight, wisdom, and good humor is Gregg Kleiner's *Where River Turns to Sky*.[7] In this story, eighty-year-old George Castor's unmarried, no-good but wealthy lawyer son, Jason, is killed in a drunk-driving automobile accident, and George inherits his son's money. He decides to leave the farmhouse he and his late wife, Dora, lived in and move into the small Oregon community near where he has lived for so many years.

George buys a big old house in the middle of town, and he and his dog, Shag William, move in. George plows up part of the formerly expansive lawn and plants a vegetable garden. Then he has the old house painted red. "Red's a color that stands up and shouts," George says. "Gets the blood going."[8] Next, he posts signs in the local nursing home inviting anyone to join him to live in the old house.

One of the first takers from the nursing home is Clara Paulson. Clara is an ex-Catholic and a former Las Vegas singer and piano player. As a young woman, Clara gave birth to a baby girl whom she gave up for adoption. She named the baby Amy and can't forget her. Unable to speak, and confined to a wheelchair by a stroke, Clara wants nothing more than to be able to sing again.

"I'd like to sing today," Clara thinks. "Sing. Somebody else could play the piano, if I could only just sing, hear my own voice coming out of me again. Words to music. I'd settle for a single song just one time through. *Singing in the Rain*.

"I miss my voice...."[9]

George Castor and Clara Paulson alternate as narrator for the story. First you get George's perspective, then Clara's, back and forth. Throughout, you live inside the hearts and minds of a little group of old people who decided to reclaim power over their own lives.

When it comes to the Fourth Commandment, that's the entire point: When we are adults ourselves, to help our parents feel that we honor and respect them. Even if they were never perfect parents—and whose parents are?—to honor and respect them, all the same. That's the point of the Fourth Commandment entirely.

Notes

1. *Catechism of the Catholic Church,* n. 2197.
2. See Raymond E. Brown, S.S., *An Introduction to the New Testament* (New York: Doubleday, 1997), 620.
3. Roland de Vaux, *Ancient Israel,* Vol. 1: *Social Institutions* (New York: McGraw Hill, 1961), 39.
4. For a good popular discussion, see James Kenny, Ph.D., *Loving & Learning: A Guide to Practical Parenting* (Cincinnati: St. Anthony Messenger Press, 1992), 159–161.
5. For an excellent popular discussion, see Monica and Bill Dodds, *Caring for Your Aging Parent: A Guide for Catholic Families* (Huntington, IN: Our Sunday Visitor Publishing Division, 1997).
6. Extraordinary situations are another matter, of course. When alcoholism, other self-destructive addictions or behaviors, spousal abuse, and so on, enter into the picture, "honor" and "respect" take on meanings that may not be immediately apparent. In such cases, adult offspring need to listen well to the advice of counselors and other professionals.
7. Gregg Kleiner, *Where River Turns to Sky* (New York: Avon Books, 1996; mass market paperback edition).
8. Kleiner, ibid., 77.
9. Kleiner, ibid., 31.

Chapter 6

THE FIFTH
COMMANDMENT

Catechetical Formula

You shall not kill.

Scriptural Version

You shall not murder.
EXODUS 20:13

I n its ancient Israelite context, the Fifth Commandment
may seem wildly improbable. Here is this commandment from God, for heaven's sake, directly ordering,
point-blank, that "you shall not kill," yet the Old Testament includes many stories where killing goes on almost as
a matter of course, and everyone seems to take it for granted.
Whole armies are slaughtered on the battlefield, entire families are put to the sword, and all with God's approval (for
example, in Num 21:34–45). Cain slays Abel (Gen 4:8).
For his own selfish purposes, David sends Uriah the Hittite

into the front ranks of his army knowing that Uriah will be killed (2 Sam 11:15).

Cain lived before God gave Moses the Ten Commandments, it's true. Still, even then God's response when Cain murders Abel is definitely negative:

> And the LORD said, "What have you done? Listen; your brother's blood is crying out to me from the ground! And now you are cursed from the ground, which has opened its mouth to receive your brother's blood from your hand. When you till the ground, it will no longer yield to you its strength; you will be a fugitive and a wanderer on the earth" (Gen 4:10–12).

But what about all the killing that goes on even after Moses receives the Ten Commandments? Had none of these people, including David, ever heard about the Fifth Commandment? At times murder and mayhem are practically a way of life in the Old Testament. What gives?

We can only hypothesize that ancient Israel was no better at understanding the Fifth Commandment than the whole human race has been since then. Down through the centuries, Fifth Commandment or no Fifth Commandment, killing—"for good reasons," of course—has been a significant occupation on the part of all humanity. "You shall not kill," the commandment says, but we surround these four simple, straightforward words with rank upon rank of qualifications, of "ifs," "ands," and "buts," "unless this," and "unless that." We do all we can to think of ways to disregard "You shall not kill."

JESUS RADICALIZES THE FIFTH COMMANDMENT

In the Gospel of Matthew, Jesus leaves no doubt about where he stands on the issue of killing. He not only repeats the Fifth Commandment, he radicalizes it, making even what seem to us like lesser evils just as objectionable:

> You have heard that it was said to those of ancient times, "You shall not murder"; and "whoever murders shall be liable to judgment." But I say to you that if you are angry with a brother or sister, you will be liable to judgment; and if you insult a brother or sister, you will be liable to the council; and if you say, "You fool," you will be liable to the hell of fire. So when you are offering your gift at the altar, if you remember that your brother or sister has something against you, leave your gift there before the altar and go; first be reconciled to your brother or sister, and then come and offer your gift (Mt 5:21–24).

Matthew's Jesus not only teaches that killing is out of the question, he adds that anger and insults are strictly forbidden too. He carries this so far as to insist that human reconciliation is a prerequisite to the worship of God. There is no question about where Jesus stands on the question of killing. As far as he is concerned, to kill even a murderer is out of the question. Period. End of discussion.

Some religious traditions—the Amish and Mennonites among the most prominent—rediscovered this "radical" perspective on killing hundreds of years ago. They were, until the Vietnam War era in the late 1960s, thought by most mainline Christian churches to be pacifist kooks who refused to defend their country in time of war; "bleeding-heart liberals" who did not believe in capital punishment when it was obvious to "everyone else" that the only just punishment for some crimes was to forfeit one's own life. We might imagine God saying, not without sarcasm in his voice, "What part of 'You shall not kill' do you not understand?"

CAPITAL PUNISHMENT

In the waning years of the twentieth century, the Catholic Church has finally discovered the wisdom of the Amish and Mennonite view, at least when it comes to capital punishment. Typically, the official Catholic teaching sidles up to the issue and says something by not saying something, but here it is, the "modification" of the *Catechism of the Catholic Church* promulgated by Pope John Paul II on September 8, 1997:

> Assuming that the guilty party's identity and responsibility have been fully determined, the traditional teaching of the Church does not exclude recourse to the death penalty, if this is the only possible way of effectively defending human lives against the unjust aggressor.
>
> If, however, nonlethal means are sufficient to defend and protect people's safety from the aggressor, authority will limit itself to such means, as these are more in keeping with the concrete conditions of the common good and more in conformity with the dignity of the human person.
>
> Today, in fact, as a consequence of the possibilities which the state has for effectively preventing

crime, by rendering one who has committed an offense incapable of doing harm—without definitely taking away from him the possibility of redeeming himself—the cases in which the execution of the offender is an absolute necessity "are very rare, if not practically nonexistent."[1]

SELF-DEFENSE AND THE FIFTH COMMANDMENT

The Fifth Commandment against killing is still taken most radically by groups such as the Amish, who reject even the idea of killing in self-defense. Such traditions teach that divine revelation occurs only in the Scriptures, so those who embrace these traditions find themselves with no choice but to reject killing in all its forms no matter what the reason.

Catholicism, on the other hand, teaches that when it comes to making choices of this and many other kinds, we need to consult the God-given human capacity to reason and think. In other words, the brains God gave us can be a source of divine revelation too. Thus, Catholicism teaches that killing in self-defense is acceptable because one has the right to preserve one's own life when threatened by an aggressor.

The *Catechism of the Catholic Church* explains that, in fact, the principle of self-defense does not violate the Fifth Commandment. This is so because, in the words of Saint Thomas Aquinas, "The act of self-defense can have a double effect: the preservation of one's own life; and the killing of the aggressor....The one is intended, the other is not."[2] This is a perfect example of Catholicism's belief in human reason as a source of divine revelation to be consulted in conjunction with Scripture.

THE PRINCIPLE OF PROTECTING LIFE IN ALL ITS FORMS

Anyone who has not been living under a cabbage leaf for the last few decades knows, however, that there are more issues related to the Fifth Commandment than capital punishment and participation in wars, and most of them are subjects of hot debate. Abortion and euthanasia are only two of the most obvious. Several centuries before Christ, Moses strode down from his mountain, stone tablets in his arms, and announced, "You shall not kill." But people of the twenty-first century A.D. have some questions.

"So, Moses, wouldn't it be a mercy to 'help' someone who is terminally ill and suffering terribly to die?"

"So, Moses, wouldn't it be fine with God if someone who is terminally ill commits suicide?"

"Isn't abortion sometimes the best choice for all concerned, like if the baby is going to be severely handicapped, mentally and physically?"

"Moses, wouldn't it be a good idea if someone who is old, feeble, and tired of living could go to a clinic and ask to be euthanized so as to not be a burden on anyone else?"

"What about all the old people, and all the severely mentally and physically handicapped people? They're such a drain on society, they don't contribute anything, and they don't seem to be happy. Don't you think they should be quietly euthanized, Moses?"

"Oh, and Moses, do you think the Fifth Commandment applies in any way to 'harvesting' body parts from fetuses to be used to save the lives of babies already born?"

If Moses were around to hear such questions, his head would be spinning. In fact, old Moses may be spinning in his grave there in the "valley in the land of Moab" (Deut

34:6) in response to the fact that such questions and issues exist at all today. We, however, cannot avoid them, and pretending that they don't exist will not make them go away. The Fifth Commandment must be interpreted and applied in any situation where the death of human beings is involved.

"Another thing, Moses. Some people say that we shouldn't kill animals, either, for food or for animal fur to make coats out of, and so forth. Some people object to using animal hides to make leather for shoes, leather garments, and upholstery. Does the Fifth Commandment apply only to humans, or does it refer to animals, too? Moses? Moses? Are you there?"

Whole tomes and countless gallons of ink have already been used to debate life-and-death issues such as these. We are not about to settle them all, clear them all up, in a few pages here. The most we can hope to do is reflect on some of the basic values involved. To begin with, if the Fifth Commandment is about anything, it's about life. When the Fifth Commandment declares, "You shall not kill," the purpose of these words is to protect life because life is from the Creator who alone can create life.

Because life is sacred, the Fifth Commandment declares that we may never directly and intentionally kill another human being. According to Church teaching, this commandment also says that we may never do anything meant to even *indirectly* cause someone's death. This includes refusing or even neglecting to help someone in danger. If a disastrous famine strikes a country on the other side of the world, for example, the Fifth Commandment requires other countries to provide assistance; to neglect giving assistance is "a scandalous injustice and a grave offense."[3]

From its early days the Christian community declared that abortion was a violation of the Fifth Commandment. The *Didache* is a nonscriptural Christian document with

Jewish roots from as early as the middle of the first century.[4] This ancient Christian document declares that, "You shall not kill the embryo by abortion and shall not cause the newborn to perish."[5]

A SPECIAL REVERENCE FOR THE SICK AND DISABLED

The Fifth Commandment also has implications that don't seem to have much to do with killing. For example, in its commentary on the Fifth Commandment, the *Catechism of the Catholic Church* teaches that special respect is due those who are weakened or diminished. "Sick or handicapped persons should be helped to lead lives as normal as possible."[6] This may sound like a rather obvious, even innocuous admonition, but just think about the practical implications.

Many parishes, for example, need to take more seriously the need to help parishioners with handicaps "lead lives as normal as possible" in the context of parish life. Are there ramps for easy access to the parish church for those who use wheelchairs or electric carts? What about in the church itself? People who use wheelchairs or electric carts are often ready to serve as extraordinary ministers of the eucharist or lectors, but they need to have accommodations made in the sanctuary area so they can get around.

Steps and stairs of all kinds can be an insurmountable obstacle for someone in a wheelchair or electric cart. Yet many parishes that have ramps into the church itself resist installing ramps in and around the sanctuary area. Quite often, this can be done in a way that blends well with already existing sanctuary construction. Certainly at times when a church interior is to be remodeled, the needs of handicapped parishioners must be taken into account.

Sometimes the question, "What would Jesus do?" can be an exercise in simplemindedness, but in this case it is precisely the question to ask. If Jesus were the pastor of this parish, or the head of the parish council, would he install ramps in the sanctuary area for those in wheelchairs or electric carts? The answer, obviously, is yes. Why? Because the church interior exists for people, people don't exist for the church interior. Because, in the spirit of the Fifth Commandment, to do so is to promote and respect life.

Finally, one of the most difficult and painful experiences related to the Fifth Commandment is suicide. When it comes to the attitude you cultivate toward your own life, it is essential to understand that we receive the gift of life from God, so we do not "own" this life in the sense that we can dispose of it any time we wish.[7] Suicide contradicts proper love for self, and it violates love for neighbor because it harms relationships with family, friends, and even with the wider society.

When someone takes his or her own life, it often leaves loved ones in anguish. Is suicide not a clear violation of the Fifth Commandment? Prior to the Second Vatican Council, in the mid 1960s, official Catholic teaching left the relatives of those who died by suicide with little hope for his or her eternal destiny. "It is the law of the Church," said the *Baltimore Catechism*, "that the bodies of those who have knowingly and deliberately committed suicide shall not be given a Christian burial."[8]

Today, however, psychological insights enable Catholic teaching to be more understanding and compassionate. According to the *Catechism of the Catholic Church*, no one should ever despair concerning the eternal salvation of those who commit suicide.[9]

The Fifth Commandment forbids murder, but its implications are far deeper and wider than it would appear. The

Fifth Commandment is about life and the preservation of life, so that whenever we celebrate life, cultivate life, and protect life we observe the Fifth Commandment.

Notes

1. *Catechism of the Catholic Church* (Modifications from the *Editio Typica*. Libreria Editrice Vaticana / United States Catholic Conference: 1997), n. 2266. The phrase in quotation marks is from John Paul II, *Evangelium vitae*, 56.
2. Saint Thomas Aquinas, *Summa Theologiae* II–II, 64, 3. *Catechism of the Catholic Church*, n. 2269.
3. *Catechism of the Catholic Church*, n. 2269.
4. See "Didache," in Richard P. McBrien, General Editor, *The HarperCollins Encyclopedia of Catholicism* (San Francisco: HarperSanFrancisco, 1995), 416.
5. Didache 2:2.
6. *Catechism of the Catholic Church*, n. 2276.
7. See *Catechism of the Catholic Church*, n. 2280.
8. *Revised Baltimore Catechism: Confraternity Edition.* (New York: Benziger Brothers, Inc., 1949), 148.
9. See *Catechism of the Catholic Church*, n. 2282–2283.

Chapter 7

THE SIXTH COMMANDMENT

Catechetical Formula

> *You shall not commit adultery.*

Scriptural Version

> *You shall not commit adultery*
> EXODUS 20:14

I n his novel, *Good Evening Mr. & Mrs. America and All the Ships at Sea*, Catholic novelist Richard Bausch tells the story of nineteen-year-old Walter Marshall in the summer of 1964. During his senior year in high school, Walter had thought he would enter the seminary and become a priest. He attended Mass and received holy Communion almost every day in order to resist the magnetism of sin. "And for Walter Marshall, there was really only one sin, one offense of heaven that he was always trying to fortify himself against: the sin of lust. The immense tide of impure thoughts and desires that seemed always about to engulf him."[1]

For Walter Marshall, there was really only one commandment, the Sixth Commandment which, in effect, covered all sexual sins. Richard Baush's description reflects with smiling poignance the experience typical of many adolescent Catholic boys (and girls) prior to the Second Vatican Council, in the mid 1960s:

In the days before he had read the works of Thomas Merton and others, it seemed to [Walter] that the rest of the commandments were easy. In his innocence, he had seldom given them a thought: It took no effort at all to refrain from using the Lord's name; to keep from bearing false witness, or killing anyone, or adoring another God, or stealing what did not belong to him. These matters seemed settled by something in his nature: It was just not in him to do harm to anyone or anything. But the very fact of sex made him weak. It had gotten so bad that, sitting in the front pew of the church during Mass, he had even had thoughts about the nuns, their...very difference from him. These thoughts went through him before he could quite manage to unthink them, and though he worked very hard not to indulge himself (for he knew that would be the sin), each one left its residue in his heart, as though every impulse were only part of a heavy chain whose slow forging would eventually pull him down.[2]

As interpreted by Catholic moralists prior to Vatican II, the Sixth Commandment included more than adultery. It was about avoiding anything having to do with sex outside of marriage. There was really only one sin, and it was sex, unless you were married. Reading "the works of Thomas Merton and others" made the difference for Walter, and the same may be said for countless other Catholics.

NOT SO MUCH AVOIDANCE
AS ACCEPTANCE

Merton, the famous Trappist monk and author who died in 1968, wrote books that eschewed the unbalanced moralism of pre-Vatican II Catholic piety, that presented faith—loving intimacy with God, not scrupulous, legalistic moralism—as the heart of Catholic faith and spirituality.

Merton represented the radical perspective of Jesus, who says in the Gospel of Matthew, "You have heard that it was said, 'You shall not commit adultery.' But I say to you that everyone who looks at a woman with lust has already committed adultery with her in his heart (Mt 5:27–28). Merton insisted that the heart of the Christian life was not *avoiding* things, sex included, but *accepting them the right way*. He wrote:

> The first step in the interior life, nowadays, is not, as some might imagine, learning *not* to see and taste and hear and feel things. On the contrary, what we must do is begin by unlearning our wrong ways of seeing, tasting, feeling, and so forth, and acquire a few of the right ones.[3]

The *Catechism of the Catholic Church* continues the tradition of understanding the Sixth Commandment as embracing human sexuality as a whole. But it highlights the radical perspective of Jesus, explaining that the entire human person is sexual, body and soul. In particular, the catechism says, our sexuality has to do with our capacity to love and be loved and our capacity for friendship.[4]

Taken in its broadest sense, the Sixth Commandment is about the virtue of chastity, which may be best understood today as referring to integrity. In other words, the chaste person preserves the unity and wholeness of the human capacity for life and love. For the dominant popular culture, chastity has the ring of prudery about it, as if the chaste person is cold, rigid, and bound by sexual hang-ups. On the contrary, the genuinely chaste person is whole, healthy, and above all *free*.

CHASTITY AS VOCATION

Chastity takes appropriate forms depending on a person's vocation, or calling. In truth, we humans must *learn* chastity, and it's a lifelong process. Adolescents learn chastity by learning to accept and respect their sexuality and their capacity for friendship. With members of the complementary sex, learning chastity means learning to enjoy friendship in the context of affection and respect. Learning chastity in the context of a culture that thinks of adolescents as uncontrollable sexual dynamos is not easy, but it is perfectly possible.

Young adults learn chastity by growing in self-reliance, by participation in the life of a local faith community, and by a joyful respect for and acceptance of the gift of sexuality both in themselves and in others. Young adulthood is a time to grow up in every sense of the term. Instead of capitulating to the dominant popular culture, accepting it as infallible, and taking all its cues as governing the best ways to live, young adults who take their Christian faith to heart will learn about the countercultural dimension of the gospel.

Single unmarried adults will live the virtue of chastity by accepting celibacy—either temporary or permanent—as a gift, a gift that gives them the liberty to be for others ways that married people do not have the time to exercise. Chastity in the single life is celibate chastity, which does not give one permission to become an emotional recluse but, rather, gives one permission to live in a warm and caring manner with many people. Some choose to remain unmarried, others simply find that this is the way their life turns out. In both cases, chastity liberates the person to love and care for others in ways unavailable to married folks.

Those who are not yet married, but considering marriage or engaged to be married, have a special challenge to face in our time. The dominant popular culture is blasé about the widespread practice of cohabitation or "living together." Studies indicate that, in fact, consistent with the wisdom of the Christian tradition, cohabitation prior to marriage can be and often is disastrous. "Living together" can be the best way to wreck a perfectly good relationship that could possibly have led to a healthy marriage. It is a statistical fact that couples who cohabit prior to marriage have a fifty percent higher divorce rate than couples who do not live together before marriage.[5]

Chastity during courtship and the engagement period precludes sexual intercourse so the couple may grow closer in essential, nongenital ways. Couples who care about the quality of their future marriage will reject the widespread acceptance of cohabitation as a viable option and the myth that "living together" is a superior way to prepare for marriage. At time goes by, one of the most noticeable characteristics of sincere Catholic faith among young people may become the rejection of cohabitation prior to marriage.

In all cases, chastity is the virtue through which our sexuality is directed to its proper place in our life. In order to live a chaste life, regardless of age or whether you are single and celibate or married and sexually active, you try to integrate your sexuality into your life and personality in ways compatible with your state in life. It's as simple as that. The virtue of chastity shows reverence for our sexuality; it always keeps sexuality and love together. In other words, it honors the fact that our sexuality is a *relational* dimension of who we are.

Chastity is a countercultural virtue, no question about it. We live in a culture that trivializes sex, and the chaste person chooses instead to honor and dignify sex. In a culture that escapes into euphemisms when it comes to sexual sin, Catholicism insists on calling a spade a spade. Movies and television sitcoms frequently fantasize, romanticize, and trivialize what the Scriptures call "fornication," sexual intercourse between an unmarried man and woman. Fornication is wrong because it is "contrary to the dignity of persons and of human sexuality...."[6]

Sex is the symbolic acting out of the total gift of oneself and one's entire life to the other in marriage. Until a man and woman make this gift of themselves to each other formally and in public it is not yet total; therefore to have sexual intercourse prior to marriage is a lie and little more than self-indulgence, no matter how much the couple may attempt to justify their actions by rationalizing. Sex is appropriate only in a loving marriage, and a loving marriage not only allows but encourages and celebrates sex.

For a healthy marriage, sex is not just the icing on the cake, something extra. Rather, loving sex is at once the most physical and the most spiritual way husband and wife express their love for each other. Chastity in marriage means making time to make love regularly because in a relatively healthy marriage—not to say "perfect," since no perfect marriages exist between imperfect human beings—sex is a source of divine grace for the marriage. Just as they receive holy Communion repeatedly as a source of God's love and grace, so the married couple makes love often for the same reason. Sex in marriage is a sacramental experience, one that nourishes the couple's union with each other and with Christ.

A BROADER MEANING

The roots of the Sixth Commandment's meaning for today are in the Hebrew Scriptures, of course, where the commandment's meaning is limited to a prohibition of both adultery and fornication. Today we understand the Sixth Commandment to imply a need to respect human sexuality and its place in human relationships. For ancient Israel, innocent of modern psychological insights, the meaning of the Sixth Commandment was much narrower and more legalistic.

The Sixth Commandment occurs between prohibitions of murder and stealing, acts which harm one's neighbor. Leviticus 18:20 says as follows: "You shall not have sexual relations with your kinsman's wife, and defile yourself with her," thus including adultery among the sins against marriage.[7]

In ancient Israel, if a man committed adultery with a married woman, both were to be put to death (Lev 20:10 and Deut 22:22). A girl engaged to be married was treated the same as a woman already married (Deut 22:23ff), since she was her fiancé's possession just as a married woman was her husband's possession. The penalty was death by either stoning or burning.[8]

In Genesis 38:24, Judah directs that his daughter-in-law Tamar be burned alive because he suspects that she has had sex with a man while recently the widow of his son, Er, and thus promised to his other son, Shelah.[9]

The Book of Proverbs places adultery on the same level

as prostitution: "For a prostitute is a deep pit; an adulteress is a narrow well" (Prov 23:27). At the same time, it was not considered adultery for a man to have sex with prostitutes. Proverbs 29:3 declares, however, that "to keep company with prostitutes is to squander one's substance."

A husband is exhorted to be faithful to his wife (Prov 5:15–19), but if he is unfaithful he shall be punished only if he violates the rights of another man by having sex with the other man's wife. The wife, on the other hand, could expect severe punishment for sexual misconduct. A woman's husband could pardon her, but he could also divorce her and leave her disgraced.

As far as unmarried women were concerned, the consequences of sexual misbehavior of an unmarried woman is mentioned in Leviticus 21:9: if a priest's daughter becomes a prostitute the punishment was being burned alive.

Clearly, the ancient Israelites were not working with a cultural or religious model of male-female relationships based on assumptions about the equality of the sexes. Given our different cultural and religious assumptions, which presuppose both male-female equality and the uniqueness of each sex, we can say that anything the Old Testament says is wrong for men is also wrong for women, and vice-versa. Of course, the punishments dictated by the Old Testament became inappropriate many centuries ago.

As far as a strict reading of the Sixth Commandment is concerned, and apart from all that we said above about the implications of this commandment for human sexual behavior in general, we can say that the Sixth Commandment forbids both adultery—sex on the part of a married person with someone to whom he or she is not married—and fornication, sex between single, unmarried persons. The point is not that there is merely something "wrong" with adultery and fornication, or that both are sinful in an abstract, legalistic sense. The point is that, in the end, both lead to misery on the part of all concerned, and in the long run both are destructive to human relationships.

In other words, the Sixth Commandment reflects the experience of countless generations: adultery and fornication, by the very nature of the acts, harm human relationships and result in pain and unhappiness for all concerned.

Notes

1. Richard Bausch, *Good Evening Mr. & Mrs. America and All the Ships At Sea* (New York: HarperPerennial, 1997), 110.
2. Bausch, 110.
3. Thomas Merton, *No Man Is an Island* (New York: Harcourt, Brace & Co., 1955), 33.
4. See *Catechism of the Catholic Church*, n. 2332.
5. One of the best resources for information on cohabitation is a video cassette: Barbara Markey, Ph.D., *Preparing Cohabitating Couples for Marriage* (FOCCUS, Inc., 3214 N. 60th St., Omaha, NE 68104; phone 402/551–9003). The selected bibliography in the Study Guide that comes with this video provides ample evidence for the extensive research carried out on the effects of cohabitation prior to marriage.
6. *Catechism of the Catholic Church*, n. 2353.
7. See Roland de Vaux, *Ancient Israel* I:36.
8. See Roland de Vaux, *Ancient Israel* I:36.
9. The law of levirate dictated that if a man died childless his brother was to have sex with his brother's widow so that the dead man would have children to carry on his name.

Chapter 8

THE SEVENTH COMMANDMENT

Catechetical Formula

You shall not steal.

Scriptural Version

You shall not steal.
EXODUS 20:15

There was a time when teachers and catechists required school children to memorize the Ten Commandments and be able to recite them at the drop of a hat. If there was one commandment that no child had trouble understanding it was this one: "You shall not steal." The meaning of these words was perfectly clear. You should never take something that does not belong to you. Still, as with most of the commandments, the meaning and implications are wider than any child could ever suspect.

ENSLAVEMENT OF MANY KINDS

Old Testament scholars suspect that the original meaning of "You shall not steal" in Exodus 20:15 condemned the seizure of a free person to make him or her a slave.[1] This interpretation gathers support from the fact that the Ninth and Tenth Commandments are much more explicit about not going after other people's possessions. What could the original meaning of "You shall not steal" possibly mean in a contemporary context? Most people today are, after all, not tempted to force someone else into slavery...unless, of course, we take a closer look at the meaning of "slavery."

Are there any forms of slavery that are common today, to which the Seventh Commandment may apply? More to the point, are there any ways today that people lead other people into chains of one kind or another, metaphorically speaking? In fact, it doesn't take a rocket scientist to see ways that this happens every day. One difference between today and Old Testament times is that today people often lead others into slavery through the power of impersonal multinational corporations.

Slavery today is a business, not a one-on-one personal matter. Also, the slavery is more emotional, economic, and spiritual than physical. In Old Testament times a man or woman might become a prisoner of war and then find himself or herself a slave in the household of a wealthy family. Today, in our culture, the "war" is waged by corporate interests, and at stake are the hearts, minds, bodies, and souls of countless people who are victimized by these corporate interests and their insatiable thirst for profits.

One of the most common examples of how corporations seize people today and carry them off into slavery is the tobacco industry's dedication to the spread and cultivation of nicotine addiction. Addiction to nicotine causes hundreds of thousands of deaths every year, yet the tobacco industry continues in business with no qualms of conscience on the part of corporate leaders and their employees. The cigarette companies target children and adolescents with mass media advertising, and the tobacco industry's hundreds of highly paid lawyers continue to help tobacco interests sidestep legal and financial accountability, tying up the courts with interminable lawsuits. Tobacco industry lawyers insist that people freely choose to smoke for the pleasure of smoking. They fail to point out that the only "pleasure" smokers experience is the "pleasure" they get when they smoke another cigarette to get relief from the discomfort of going into withdrawal from their addiction.

People suffer a slow, agonizing death by the hundreds of thousands each year from illnesses directly related to slavery to nicotine. This is a blatant violation of the Seventh Commandment. Government too—meaning all of us—is implicated by its failure to protect citizens from the tobacco industry, which takes unfair advantage of people for the sake of financial gain.

This is one modern instance of a massive public violation of the Seventh Commandment. Other ways corporations and governments enslave people include the failure to help people overcome poverty and ignorance through economic assistance and education programs. For example, according to the results of a survey released by the U.S. Department of Education in 1993, at that time more than forty million American adults were functionally illiterate.[2] This is a form of slavery that witnesses to yet another social violation of the Seventh Commandment.

People remain enslaved by poverty and a lack of education, in many cases because the rest of us benefit from their enslavement. As long as there are people who are poor and ignorant, we will have people to take low-paying, menial jobs. Even in its original meaning, then, the Seventh Commandment has relevance today, if only we are willing to look around and take responsibility for the kinds of slavery that exist in our time and place.

RESPECT FOR THE RIGHTS OF ALL

In its modern application, of course, the Seventh Commandment also insists that it is sinful to take and keep anything that rightfully belongs to someone else. According to the *Catechism of the Catholic Church*, this commandment directs us to "justice and charity" in the care of all goods of this earth and the fruits of human labor.[3] This includes respect for the human right to private property. At the same time, the right to private property does not eliminate the fact that God gave the earth to all of humankind. The ownership of private property carries with it the responsibility to care for that property with the needs and rights of all people in mind.

The Seventh Commandment directly opposes greed or the immoderate accumulation of material possessions. Carried to its logical conclusion, the Seventh Commandment encourages the practice of simplicity in all things. Most of us need far less than we think we need and accumulate far more than we have a right to. This is particularly true in a world where international economic and social inequalities are so obvious and so great.

In summary, the *Catechism of the Catholic Church* teaches that the Seventh Commandment

> ...forbids acts or enterprises that for any reason—
> selfish or ideological, commercial, or totalitarian—
> lead to the enslavement of human beings, to their
> being bought, sold, and exchanged like merchandise,

in disregard for their personal dignity. It is a sin against the dignity of persons and their fundamental rights to reduce them by violence to their productive value or to a source of profit.[4]

Obviously, the Seventh Commandment forbids outright stealing. At the same time, Catholicism insists that common sense, too, can be a source of divine revelation. God gave us brains, and he expects us to use them. Therefore, it is not stealing when, for example, in cases of urgent need people take from others in order to meet essential requirements for food, shelter, and clothing. When this happens, however, a society needs to ask itself about failures to provide for those who are economically disadvantaged, failures which, in themselves, could easily be violations of the Seventh Commandment.

SOCIAL AND ECONOMIC IMPLICATIONS

Closely related to observance of the Seventh Commandment are the virtues of temperance, justice, and solidarity. The Seventh Commandment requires us to practice temperance, which helps us to control our attachment to material goods. The average North American accumulates a mountain of possessions compared to people in most other parts of the world. Not only that, but we have an economic system that depends on constantly pressuring people, through mass media advertising, to accumulate more, and more, and still more. In this cultural context, there is no such thing as "enough."

To observe the Seventh Commandment, we also need to practice the virtue of justice. This virtue helps us to respect and preserve other people's rights and give them what they have a right to. Employers owe employees a living wage, and employees owe employers an honest day's work for that wage. In a society where more and more people have no medical insurance, where politicians and for-profit medical care systems battle daily, the simple human need for medical care hangs in midair. Is medical care a basic human right? Does the Seventh Commandment require societies and governments to not "steal" medical care from people by withholding it from them?

The *Catechism of the Catholic Church* lists other examples of social evils that violate the Seventh Commandment, including speculation in order to artificially manipulate the price of goods to gain an advantage over others; corruption in order to influence the judgment of anyone who must make decisions according to the law; stealing from one's employer or from government agencies; doing work poorly that one is hired to do; any form of tax evasion; forgery of any kind; and purposely damaging private or public property.[5]

The implications of the Seventh Commandment are broad, indeed. This commandment applies to everything from promises made to contracts agreed on and signed. Once again, of course, Catholicism's understanding of this commandment is anything but simplistic. If it turns out that any part of a contract is unfair or unjust, the persons signing it are not bound to keep that part of the contract.

Why is it important to include promises and contracts in our understanding of the Seventh Commandment? Because the economic and social life of a given community depends, in large part, on people keeping their promises and acting in accordance with the contracts they sign. If people stop keeping their promises and fail to live up to their contracts, the social and economic life of a society will soon disintegrate.

The Seventh Commandment also applies to the earth

and its natural resources. We may not seize the earth's resources in a way that leaves the earth barren or causes irreparable damage. Human dominion over the earth requires us to care for the interests of our neighbors, including people who will live on the earth long after we are gone. The *Catechism* insists that we are to have "a religious respect for the integrity of creation."[6]

Catholic tradition contributes wisdom to today's ecological and environmental concerns. When the Seventh Commandment declares that we are not to steal, Catholicism even applies this to human interest in animals.[7] Animals are created by God, and they reflect the divine beauty and goodness. Saints such as Saint Francis of Assisi (c. 1181–1226), Saint Philip Neri (1515–1595), and Saint John Bosco (1815–1888) treated animals with extraordinary kindness, and their example should guide our actions today.

At the same time, Catholicism believes that humans have stewardship over animals. According to the Book of Genesis:

> God blessed Noah and his sons, and said to them, "Be fruitful and multiply, and fill the earth. The fear and dread of you shall rest on every animal of the earth, and on every bird of the air, on everything that creeps on the ground, and on all the fish of the sea; into your hand they are delivered. Every moving thing that lives shall be food for you; and just as I gave you the green plants, I give you everything" (Gen 9:1–3).

Therefore, it is perfectly legitimate to use animals for food and clothing, and animals may be used for work and leisure. Even medical and scientific experimentation on animals is acceptable, if it is carried out in reasonable ways, since it is done to help improve and/or save human lives. It is, however, contrary to the Seventh Commandment to cause animals to suffer or die out of neglect, cruelty, or for no real purpose. At the same time, it is wrong to spend money on animals when human needs take precedence.

A final word about animals, particularly when they are used as pets. It is fine for people to love their pets. But no one should give animals the love or affection that should go only to other persons. People who substitute pets for people are misguided; if you seem to lack people in your life that may be a call to reach out to others rather than withdraw into your own little "cocoon" with a couple of cats and a dog. There are people who need you.

Catholicism finds in the Seventh Commandment the seeds of a perspective that encompasses human life and human societies taken together. In the Seventh Commandment we find inspiration for social and economic doctrines that seek justice and fairness for all concerned. Here we find the seeds of the Church's rejection of any world view that would govern societies by nothing but economic factors. Thus, any philosophy that would make profit the only standard and the ultimate goal of business is immoral.[8]

Any social or economic system that views people as nothing but "consumers" thinks, in effect, that people are slaves to economics. Not only is this a violation of the Seventh Commandment, but it leads to making an idol of money, a violation of the First Commandment which encourages what we might call "practical atheism."[9] For this reason, Catholicism rejects all totalitarian and atheistic philosophies and ideologies. For this reason, too, the Church wants nothing to do with an unregulated capitalism that sees profit as an end in itself and human beings as subservient to the demands of the marketplace.

The Seventh Commandment has implications for the

world of work. For example, no one should be deprived of work that pays a living wage. Men and women, those who are healthy and those with disabilities, natives and immigrants, regardless of race, ethnic background, religion, or sexual orientation, all have a right to work. Indeed, Catholic social doctrine even states that workers have a moral right to strike for the sake of justice, although violence is to be avoided.[10]

Startling though it may be, ultimately the Seventh Commandment is about...love. We are to not steal from others, and we are to not contribute in any way to the enslavement of others, because we are to love them. This is the ultimate Christian perspective on the Seventh Commandment.

THE ULTIMATE REQUIREMENT: LOVE

One of the most articulate and captivating commentators on the connections between love and social and economic perspectives was Dorothy Day (1897–1980), co-founder of the Catholic Worker movement. In her 1948 book, *On Pilgrimage*, Dorothy Day wrote:

> Whenever I groan within myself and think how hard it is to keep writing about love in these times of tension and strife, which may at any moment become for us all a time of terror, I think to myself, "What else is the world interested in?" What else do we all want, each one of us, except to love and be loved, in our families, in our work, in all our relationships? God is Love. Love casts out fear. Even the most ardent revolutionist, seeking to change the world, to overturn the tables of the money changers, is trying to make a world where it is easier for people to love, to stand in that relationship to each other.

We want with all our hearts to love, to be loved.
And not just in the family but to look upon all as
our mothers, sisters, brothers, children.[11]

This perspective of Dorothy Day sidesteps romanticism
and presents the iron-solid truth that ultimately what everyone wants more than anything else is love—and God is
love, so what we all hunger and thirst for is God. Ultimately,
the Seventh Commandment is a reminder that a life based
on anything but love is an empty life.

The Seventh Commandment also has an international
application. The wealthier nations can steal from poorer
nations in many other ways besides taking advantage of
them through political imperialism. Rich nations can steal
from poor nations by not helping when and where help is
needed. "Rich nations have a grave moral responsibility
toward those which are unable to ensure the means of their
development by themselves or have been prevented from
doing so by tragic historical events."[12]

As with stealing on an individual level, when nations
steal from other nations through omission or neglect, they
have a responsibility to make restitution. In other words,
there is much room for rich nations to help poor nations
without expecting repayment. When rich nations can for-
give the debts of poor nations to whom they have granted
loans, for example, this should be done with no need for
lengthy debate. Justice demands it, pure and simple.

A FINAL PERSPECTIVE

There is also, finally, a distinctive Christian perspective on
the Seventh Commandment that we may not overlook. The
original Hebrew understanding of this Commandment for-
bade what, in modern terms, we call kidnapping. Later

meanings attached to it were simpler and more obvious to us, namely, the belief that it is never acceptable to take from others what belongs to them. As we have seen, there are social and economic implications to this on both the individual, social, and international levels. But there is a distinctively Christian perspective on the Seventh Commandment that is personal, even subjective, as well.

When we learn that it is contrary to the will of God to deprive others of their freedom and independence, you may well apply this to yourself, as well. In other words, be aware of ways you may steal from yourself and deprive yourself of your freedom and independence. Part of a personal morality is the need to reject anything that deprives you of what you need to live a life rooted in the freedom and joy of Christ.

What are some ways you can be "kidnapped"? What are some ways you can allow faith, hope, and love to be stolen from you? Part of a healthy Christian spirituality is to be on the alert to resist anything that deprives you of your spiritual freedom to act out of faith in every dimension of your life.

Notes

1. See Roland de Vaux, *Ancient Israel* (New York: McGraw Hill, 1965), I:83.
2. This statistic is from the Internet web site of the Literacy Service of Indian River County (Florida), http: //www.indian-river.fl.us/ living/services/als/facts.html.
3. *Catechism of the Catholic Church*, n. 2401.
4. *Catechism of the Catholic Church*, n. 2414.
5. See *Catechism of the Catholic Church*, n. 2409.
6. *Catechism of the Catholic Church*, n. 2415.
7. See *Catechism of the Catholic Church*, n. 2416–2418.

8. See *Catechism of the Catholic Church*, n. 2424.

9. See Craig M. Gay, *The Way of the (Modern) World, or Why It's Tempting to Live As If God Doesn't Exist* (Grand Rapids, MI: Wm. B. Eerdmans Publishing Co., 1998).

10. See *Catechism of the Catholic Church*, n. 2435.

11. Dorothy Day, *On Pilgrimage* (Grand Rapids, MI: Wm. B. Eerdmans Publishing Co., 1999), 123.

12. *Catechism of the Catholic Church*, n. 2439.

Chapter 9

THE EIGHTH COMMANDMENT

Catechetical Formula

> *You shall not bear false witness*
> *against your neighbor.*

Scriptural Version

> *You shall not bear false witness*
> *against your neighbor.*
> EXODUS 20:16

The spirit of the Eighth Commandment is the spirit of truth. If ever there was a commandment that should ring a bell for Christians, it is this one. For Jesus says, in the Gospel of John: "If you continue in my word, you are truly my disciples; and you will know the truth, and the truth will make you free" (Jn 8:31–32). Indeed, this same gospel tells us that Jesus himself is "full of grace and truth" (Jn 1:14). Therefore, in a mystical and very real sense, to be truthful is to be united with Christ.

The original meaning of the Eighth Commandment was to make sure that only the truth would be told in the law courts of ancient Israel. Accused persons were tried at the city gates, and guilt or innocence was determined by whatever male Israelites were present.[1] Guilt could be determined based on the testimony of two witnesses, so it was essential that only the truth be told. This was particularly true since in the case of guilt the sentence was carried out immediately, and there was no chance for appeal.

THE SPIRIT OF TRUTH

With time, the meaning of the Eighth Commandment expanded to encompass truthfulness and integrity in all kinds of relationships. But no matter where we apply a concern for truth, the basis for our concern is our faith relationship with the one who *is* truth, the risen Christ. We seek truth because through our faith we are rooted in the truth.

Of course, we can act as virtuous as we want to about always wanting "the truth, the whole truth, and nothing but the truth." But if we are honest, we must admit that sometimes the truth is precisely what we do *not* want. Sometimes, after all, the truth gets in the way of our prejudices and preconceived notions. Sometimes the truth gets in the way of our opinions! And that we cannot tolerate. "Ye shall know the truth," quipped philosopher Aldous Huxley, "and the truth shall make you mad."[2]

"Truth" is a peculiar notion. Many groups, organizations, religions, philosophies, and political parties act as if they have a firm grasp on the whole truth. If you want the truth you had better belong to this group, religion, political party, because the others do *not* have the truth. In the past, popular Catholicism had a particular penchant for acting as if it had an exclusive claim to the truth. Catholics had the truth, and all those benighted others, Protestants and all those "pagans," were beyond hope.

Of course, anyone who wanted to do some looking could soon discover that Saint Thomas Aquinas (1225–1274), that most Catholic of all theologians, wrote: "Every truth without exception—and whoever may utter it—is from the Holy Spirit."[3] And Cardinal John Henry Newman (1801–1890) said: "No truth can really exist external to Christianity."[4]

In other words, the Church has no exclusive claim on the truth. Not only that, but if Catholicism would be faithful to the best in its own tradition it needs to be open to truth, whatever its source. That means other religions and philosophies, the arts, the world of commerce, and the experience and insights even of atheists and agnostics. The Dalai Lama—worldwide leader of Tibetan Buddhism—is just as likely to speak truth as the Pope.

Of course, we can't expect the Dalai Lama to speak from the fullness of Christian revelation. Still, when he speaks the truth, the fact that the truth he speaks lacks the Christian dimension and a Christian perspective and is therefore incomplete, does not mean that what he says is therefore untrue. Rather, the truth the Dalai Lama speaks is at the most completely true, at the least incompletely true, depending on the topic. But what he says is true in either case. It is perfectly possible that the Dalai Lama—or an atheist philosopher, or a Hindu guru, or an agnostic artist, or a Unitarian—could speak aspects of human and spiritual truths that Catholics may have overlooked recently. The fact that the reminder comes from someone outside the Catholic tradition makes no difference; it is still the truth, and Catholicism welcomes that truth with open arms. To refuse to do so would be contrary to the Eighth Commandment.

In the Gospel of John, when Jesus declares before Pilate that he "came into the world, to testify to the truth" (Jn 18:37a), he places himself squarely on the side of truth regardless of its source. While it may be easy to apply this in theory, of course, on a daily basis the most critical need is to apply it to our most everyday encounters and relationships. We may be tempted to speak ill of someone, for example, when our words will damage another's reputation. To do this would be to "bear false witness."

THE CHALLENGE OF SPEAKING WELL OF OTHERS

The *Catechism of the Catholic Church* singles out three ways we can violate the Eighth Commandment with regard to others:[5]

1. *Rash Judgment.* This means you accept as true, without sufficient evidence, that someone else did something morally wrong.
2. *Detraction.* Without any objectively valid reason, you tell someone about another person's faults and failings.
3. *Calumny.* By making comments that are not true, you harm someone's reputation and give others cause to form a false opinion of him or her.

One alternative that covers all of the above was articulated by Saint Ignatius Loyola in the sixteenth century in his famous *Spiritual Exercises*:

Every good Christian ought to be more ready to give a favorable interpretation to another's statement than to condemn it. But if he cannot do so, let him ask how the other understands it. And if the latter understands it badly, let the former correct him with love. If that does not suffice, let the Christian try all suitable ways to bring the other to a correct interpretation so that he may be saved.[6]

The Eighth Commandment is about being truthful in one's relationships with others; therefore, it is about not telling lies in any form. We can be highly "creative," however, in coming up with ways to act contrary to this Commandment. When we flatter or fawn upon a person, we tell that person a lie about himself or herself; when we boast or brag about ourselves, we tell others a lie. When we tell a lie, this is actually an act of violence. It deprives someone else of his or her right to know the truth. "Lying is destructive of society; it undermines trust...and tears apart the fabric of social relationships."[7]

NO ABSOLUTES

Once again, however, Catholicism takes an approach to the Eighth Commandment that respects the complexity of human relationships and the many nuances of any human situation. For example, the obligation to tell the truth is never absolute. Love can, and frequently does, require us to decide in particular situations whether or not it is appropriate to tell the truth to someone who asks for specific information. If telling the truth would be contrary to the good or safety of someone else, then love demands that we not reveal that truth. If the privacy of another person would be violated by telling the truth, then we are justified if we remain silent or limit ourselves to what the *Catechism* calls "discreet language."[8]

If scandal would be caused by telling the truth, then we

are required to maintain discretion. We are never obliged to reveal the truth to someone who has no right to know it. "Whoever betrays secrets destroys confidence, and will never find a congenial friend" (Sir 27:16).

One of the classic examples of a situation where the truth may not be revealed is in professional or religious contexts. A psychiatrist, physician, or lawyer, for example, may not reveal information revealed to him in trust, where secrecy is presumed. The only exception, says the *Catechism*, would be in unusual situations where to keep the secret would definitely cause serious harm to the one who confided the secret, to the professional person who received it, or to a third party, and where the harm can be avoided only by revealing the truth.[9]

A priest may not be required, even by legal authorities, to reveal anything told to him in the Sacrament of Reconciliation. "The sacramental seal is inviolable," says the Code of Canon Law. "Accordingly, it is absolutely wrong for a confessor in any way to betray the penitent, for any reason whatsoever, whether by word or in any other fashion."[10]

The Code of Canon Law even goes so far as to include others in the "seal of confession/secret of the sacrament of reconciliation." The very next sentence declares: "An interpreter, if there is one, is also obliged to observe this secret, as are all others who may in any way whatever have come to a knowledge of sins from a confession."[11]

MEDIA AND THE EIGHTH COMMANDMENT

The spirit of the Eighth Commandment requires us to keep our lips zipped when it comes to other people's private lives. This applies in a particularly relevant way to the media, which in our time is rarely reluctant when it comes to doing whatever it takes to attract an audience and sell advertising time. "Interference by the media in the private lives of persons engaged in political or public activity is to be condemned to the extent that it infringes upon their privacy and freedom."[12]

Journalists, in both the print and electronic media, often face difficult decisions when it comes to telling the truth. Where should a writer or television reporter stop when it comes to the privacy of individuals, for example? Television ratings may skyrocket when a television news program shows, closeup, the bodies of people killed in a tragic automobile accident, but do high ratings make it ethical to violate the privacy of the victims as well as that of their loved ones?

A newspaper columnist may have information about a politician that if printed in the newspaper will embarrass him or her and perhaps ruin the politician's career. Does the information have anything to do with the politician's abilities and responsibilities in public office? The journalist must decide, and sometimes the answers do not come easily. Sometimes the public has a right to the truth, sometimes not.

What about advertising? Where does truth end and lies begin? Apparently "real" images can tell lies about a product. How can advertisers and ad agencies sell products and services and maintain the integrity of the truth? In today's cultural environment, it isn't easy. When is a soft drink just a soft drink and not the key to the meaning of life? When is a new car just a new car and not a requirement for healthy self-esteem? When is a beer just a beer and not the way to have good friends? How can a cosmetics company advertise its products and never tell anything but the truth?

When does a cigarette become nothing more than what it is, a way to take into one's body nicotine, a dangerous, life-threatening, highly addictive drug? What happened to the truth here? There is no question that the Eighth Commandment has meaning in today's world. But how prepared are we to think about it and take it to heart? Are we prepared to take this commandment seriously even when it may have a negative impact on the profits of multinational corporations?

Artists, too, face issues of truth telling. When does a work of art tell the truth, and when does it not tell the truth? When does art become not a means to promote the truth but merely an ideological tool or a tool of outright lies? When do images of the nude human body become pornography, which is nothing but a lie? Is a work of art that few, if any, understand still a work of art, or is it just a source of confusion?

Only human beings create works of art, and only humans can ask the question about the meaning of art. The Eighth Commandment requires us to ask such questions, and it requires us to seek the truth even if we may not initially like the truth we discover. "Arising from talent given by the Creator and from man's [sic] own effort, art is a form of practical wisdom, uniting knowledge and skill, to give form to the truth of reality in a language accessible to sight or hearing."[13]

Sacred art is a unique case, and sacred art tells the truth when it carries and communicates the divine mystery of God. Sacred art becomes specifically Christian when it successfully reflects or illuminates the Christian mysteries of the Incarnation and Redemption accomplished in Christ. Some of what passes for "sacred art" is little more than religious kitsch, "art" that may do little more than reinforce a childish or sentimental piety. What does the Eighth Commandment say about such "art"? Does it evoke the truth, or does it evoke something less than the truth?

Perhaps there is more of a connection between the original ancient Israelite juridical meaning of the Eighth Commandment than we usually think there is. Christian faith requires us to be truthful in our words and in our actions. So—to recall a familiar question—if it were against the law to be a Christian, would there be enough evidence to throw you in the slammer?

Notes

1. See Thomas Poundstone, "Commandments, the Ten," in Richard P. McBrien, general editor, *The HarperCollins Encyclopedia of Catholicism* (San Francisco: HarperSanFrancisco, 1994), 333.
2. Quoted in Jon Winokur, ed., *The Portable Curmudgeon Redux* (New York: Dutton, 1992), 292.
3. Quoted in Tony Castle, *The New Book of Christian Quotations* (New York: The Crossroad Publishing Co., 1989), 244.
4. Castle, 245.
5. See *Catechism of the Catholic Church*, n. 2477.
6. Saint Ignatius of Loyola, *Spiritual Exercises*, 22. Quoted in *Catechism of the Catholic Church*, n. 2478.
7. *Catechism of the Catholic Church*, n. 2486.
8. *Catechism of the Catholic Church*, n. 2489.
9. See *Catechism of the Catholic Church*, n. 2489.
10. The Canon Law Society of Great Britain and Ireland, et al., *The Code of Canon Law in English Translation* (Grand Rapids, MI: Wm. B. Eerdmans Publishing Co., 1983), can. 983.1.
11. The Canon Law Society of Great Britain and Ireland, et al., can. 983.2.
12. *Catechism of the Catholic Church*, n. 2492.
13. *Catechism of the Catholic Church*, n. 2501.

Chapter 10

THE NINTH COMMANDMENT

Catechetical Formula

You shall not covet your neighbor's wife.

Scriptural Version

Neither shall you covet your neighbor's wife....
DEUTERONOMY 6:21A[1]

The scriptural origins of the Ninth Commandment are clearly in an ancient Israelite society and a patriarchal culture which believed women to have less dignity than men. A married woman was her husband's property; he owned her just as he owned his house, his animals, and his other possessions. At the same time, it would be a mistake to assume that the entire Old Testament has a single perspective on women. Compared to other cultures in the ancient Near East, Greece, and Rome, the legal and social position of Hebrew women was superior.

AN OLD TESTAMENT VIEW OF WOMEN

The Israelite mother is explicitly included in the precepts of honor and obedience which sons must pay to parents (Ex 20:12; Lev 19:3; Deut 5:16 and 21:18). Women participated in festive celebrations; in fact, women's songs and dancing were among the most important elements of a celebration (Ex 15:20; Judg 11:34; 1 Sam 19:11ff). Women also took part in cultic festivals (Deut 12:12; Judg 13:20–23; 1 Sam 1:1–4 and 2).

Women are among those whose stories are told because of their wisdom and devotion. These include Rahab (Josh 2), Michal (1 Sam 19:11ff), Abigail (1 Sam 25:14ff), Rizpah (2 Sam 21:7ff), and the women of Shunem (2 Kings 4:8ff). Portrayals of the wives of the patriarchs—Sarah, Hagar, Rebekah, Rachel, and Leah—and of such colorful characters as Jezebel, Delilah, and Athaliah—are more ambiguous. Still, we cannot say that these women constitute an oppressed group.

Deborah is a Hebrew heroine, and the women in the Book of Ruth are presented with all the strong qualities of womanhood. The books named for Judith and Esther tell the stories of still other heroines.[2] Finally, in the Book of Tobit, "Women are highly regarded…as persons capable of prayer (Tob 3:11–15), wage earning (Tob 2:11–12), and religious education."[3]

It is also true that Hebrew law included provisions that gave women special protection. This was true of the laws concerning the prisoner of war (Deut 21:10ff); the wife falsely charged with not being a virgin prior to marriage (Deut 22:13ff); and the girl who is raped (Deut 22:28ff). Admittedly, such laws are the exception, so "one may deduce that the position of women was guaranteed by custom rather than by law."[4]

The most significant section of the Old Testament with regard to the position of women is Chapters 2 and 3 of Genesis. Chapter 2 declares that the woman is a helper of the same species as man, "bone of his bone and flesh of his flesh." For woman, man leaves his parents and lives with his wife. This clearly implies equality, and this implication is made explicit in Genesis 3:16, where the de facto inferiority of woman, and her subjection to man, and her dependence upon him for sexual fulfillment—the source of her subjection—is said to be the result of a curse. Therefore, the inferiority of women is declared to be a corruption or deterioration from the way God designed things in the beginning.[5]

A THROWAWAY SOCIETY

Returning, however, to the main thrust of our discussion, originally the Ninth Commandment was about not coveting another man's wife precisely because she was the other man's *possession*. This may seem to be a culturally outmoded notion, especially in an era heavily influenced by feminism. If we apply the prohibition to both women and men, however, the Ninth Commandment may prove to carry more meaning for our time than we first thought.

Our culture is one that supports a "throwaway" lifestyle. The cultural standard is to use something until you get tired of it, or until it gets old, then throw it away and get a new one. The car you have accumulates a certain number of miles and you trade it in or sell it and get another one. The small appliance you bought five years ago quits functioning. Do you find someone to repair it? Of course not, it would cost more to fix the old one than to buy a new one. So you drop it in the trash can and go shopping.

Not only do we apply this attitude to material things,

but by extension we also tend to have the same attitude toward other things in life—jobs, for example. When one job gets boring, find another one. When we tire of living in one place, why not live in another place? Everything can be thrown away or left behind and replaced.

Perhaps you think it's stretching things too far to say that we also tend to have this throwaway approach to marriage? Would that you were right. Many couples enter marriage today with precisely this attitude. A couple married twenty years helped out with a marriage preparation program for engaged couples. Many engaged couples today cohabit for months or years before deciding to marry. With a small group of engaged couples, the older couple raised some questions about the wisdom of "living together" before marriage. One of the young men replied, "You wouldn't buy a pair of shoes without trying them on, would you?"

Many couples today bring the values of consumerism to their choice of a marriage partner, either consciously as this young man seems to have done, or unconsciously. The logical extension of this attitude would be to ask, "When the shoes get worn and scuffed, or you get tired of them and see another pair of shoes you would rather have, you get rid of them, right? When your wife gets older, or you get tired of her, or you see another woman you would rather have, will you discard your wife and get another one?"

The point, of course, is that a spouse is not a pair of shoes. In our time, perhaps the Ninth Commandment is about not having a throwaway attitude in marriage. Perhaps the Ninth Commandment is about not allowing yourself to entertain a "grass is always greener on the other side of the fence" attitude in marriage. Both men and women can grow tired of their spouse, can be attracted by someone else, can be tempted to scrap the old husband or wife in favor of a new one.

The Ninth Commandment says, "Hey, grow up." A spouse is not just another commodity on the shelf of life. Don't have a wandering eye. You choose one spouse—imperfect in many ways as you now realize—and you stick with him or her for life. You don't think about being married to the young hunk or dolly of your dreams. You don't fantasize about being married to someone who is already married to someone else. You remain faithful to the husband or wife you already have, warts and all. You love him or her every day. You act like a grownup. That's what the Ninth Commandment is about.

PURITY OF HEART

Flip to the appropriate pages in the *Catechism of the Catholic Church*, and you may be mystified to see that the catechism interprets the Ninth Commandment as being about the need to resist "concupiscence" and cultivate purity of heart. Imagine that. The catechism defines "concupiscence" as "any intense form of human desire... the movement of the sensitive appetite contrary to the operation of human reason....Concupiscence...unsettles [our] moral faculties and, without being in itself an offense, inclines [us] to commit sins."[6]

In other words, "concupiscence" is the condition in human nature that inclines us to make stupid/sinful choices such as thinking that someone else would make a better husband or wife. "Look at Joe's wife, she's a babe!" or "Sally's husband, he's far more caring and sensitive than the guy I'm married to. I wonder...."

The catechism recommends as a remedy for concupiscence that we cultivate purity of heart. "The struggle against carnal covetousness entails purifying the heart and practicing temperance...."[7] Then the catechism makes the obvious connection with the gospel by quoting the sixth beatitude in the Gospel of Matthew: "Blessed are the pure in heart, for they will see God" (Mt 5:8).

Purity of heart helps us to see things as God sees them. So instead of seeing in some other man or woman—perhaps someone else's husband or wife—a potential replacement for the man or woman you married, with purity of heart you see a "neighbor," in the gospel sense of the word, someone who is "a temple of the Holy Spirit" (1 Cor 6:19). You see a full, real human person with a life, and history, and future, and joys and sorrows, and commitments of his or her own. With purity of heart, you look at your own spouse and see the same—a gloriously imperfect human being who will never be a throwaway or interchangeable commodity on the shelf of life.[8]

The Ninth Commandment, as understood by Catholic tradition, implies that at the center of life is a concern for purity of heart, purity of body, and purity of faith.[9] Purity of heart enables us to see other people and ourselves in more than a superficial fashion. We become capable of seeing "with the heart" and "into the heart (of others)."

Purity of body refers to chastity, which is not the same as prudishness or puritanism. Chastity is the virtue that enables us to "love with an upright and undivided heart."[10] If you are married, chastity makes it possible to love your spouse as a real person, as nobody's fantasy, and it makes it possible for you—in normal circumstances—to have a full and joyful sex life. A chaste married couple is free to enjoy sex to the fullest because making love is basic to a spirituality of marriage and parenthood.

If you are single, chastity makes it possible for you to never be satisfied with superficial relationships with anyone. Therefore, as a single person, chastity enables you to reject the trivialized cultural perception of sex as a mere way to have a good time, with no necessary connection between sex and a lifelong commitment in marriage. For single people, chastity includes rejection of the popular but false idea that as a way to prepare for marriage cohabitation is superior to a traditional noncohabiting engagement.

Whether married or single, and regardless of age, chastity is the Christian virtue that makes it possible for us to act like grownups in all our relationships. That's the key to understanding and living the Ninth Commandment, of course: maturity and fidelity in relationships of all kinds, from the most casual acquaintance to the closest friendship, and marriage itself. To "not covet your neighbor's wife"— or husband—can be a kind of metaphorical statement. It is a negative way to make a positive statement. It's a way of saying, Be faithful in all your relationships with others in ways appropriate to each relationship.

It's true for all the commandments, but it's particularly appropriate to articulate it here. Daily prayer is basic to a life guided and enlightened by the Ninth Commandment. That way a living and lively intimacy with God our loving Father, in Christ, will condition and nourish all our relationships with other people. For our relationships with other people cannot be separated from our relationship with our Father in heaven who is closer to us than we are to ourselves.

Notes

1. Chapters 2 through 8 quoted from the version of the Decalogue in Exodus. Chapters 10 and 11 use the version of the Decalogue in Deuteronomy because it provides a clearer scriptural distinction between the two commandments.
2. See John L. McKenzie, *Dictionary of the Bible* (New York: Macmillan & Co., 1965), 936.

3. Irene Nowell, "Tobit." In Raymond E. Brown, S.S., et al., editors, *The New Jerome Biblical Commentary* (Englewood Cliffs, NJ: Prentice Hall, 1990), 569.

4. McKenzie, 936.

5. See McKenzie, 936

6. *Catechism of the Catholic Church*, n. 2515.

7. *Catechism of the Catholic Church*, n. 2517.

8. It would carry us too far off our topic to discuss in detail situations where a spouse is abusive and other similar situations, which are another case entirely.

9. See *Catechism of the Catholic Church*, n. 2518.

10. *Catechism of the Catholic Church*, n. 2520.

Chapter 11

THE TENTH COMMANDMENT

Catechetical Formula

You shall not covet your neighbor's goods.

Scriptural Version

Neither shall you desire...anything that belongs to your neighbor.

DEUTERONOMY 6:21B

On first sight, the Tenth Commandment may seem to be little more than a prohibition against wanting to possess other people's possessions. Look it up in a dictionary, however, and you'll see that *covet* is a strong word. It means "to feel blameworthy desire for (that which is another's)." The key phrase is "blameworthy desire."

A COVETOUS FRAME OF MIND

You might say that the Tenth Commandment prohibits lusting after other people's possessions. Even more to the point, the key to understanding this commandment is to see, with Jewish scholar Menachem Kellner, that coveting "is not an action, but rather a frame of mind."[1] The logical question becomes, then, What is objectionable about desire? Kellner observes that according to the great medieval Jewish philosopher Maimonides, this commandment explicitly prohibits specific thoughts and emotions. Even if we only desire possessions that belong to our neighbor, we sin.

> If one desires another's house or his wife or his goods or any similar thing that he might buy from him, he transgresses a negative commandment as soon as he thinks in his heart how he is to acquire the desired object and allows his mind to be seduced by it. For Scripture says, Nor shall you desire, and desire is a matter of the heart only.[2]

Maimonides takes quite seriously a key word in the Deuteronomic version of the Tenth Commandment, which states: "Neither shall you desire your neighbor's house, or field, or male or female slave, or ox, or donkey, or anything that belongs to your neighbor" (Deut 5:21b).

"Neither shall you *desire*...." The problem is with desiring what we do not have. The word *covet* rather than *desire* occurs in the Exodus version of the Decalogue (20:17). But here in Deuteronomy the Tenth Commandment deals a roundhouse blow to the cultural solar plexus. For the dominant Western culture depends for its survival upon covetous desire. In fact, the economy depends on people constantly desiring what they do not have.

WANTING MORE THAN WE NEED

Is the Tenth Commandment relevant today? The last thing the dominant culture and its attendant economy wants is for you to be satisifed with what you already have. The mass media advertising industry exists to get us to desire what we do not have and, in fact, to get us to desire what we do not have even though we have no need for it. Anyone who takes the Tenth Commandment seriously is bound to end up in a countercultural position, bound in conscience to cultivate a simpler lifestyle.

The ideal human condition, as far as the dominant culture is concerned, is a bizarre state of unsatisfied arousal—and I use the word *arousal* advisedly. For remember, we are talking here about desire. Typically, we use the word *arousal* to describe the process of increasing sexual desire and its physical manifestations. But "arousal" may just as easily apply to a desire for almost anything. The purpose of mass media advertising is to arouse in us a desire for things we do not have and frequently do not need. For once you are "aroused," the natural drive is toward satisfaction of your desire, and this satisfaction is accomplished, but only temporarily, by the act of purchasing the thing you desire.

We tend to live in a constant state of desire for things we do not have. This is what drives the economy! But on a personal and spiritual level, a condition of constant desire that is never fully satisfied eats away at our deepest center. This constant state of arousal that is never satisfied erodes genuine human peace and tranquillity. Even more to the point, we confuse our inborn desire for God with desires elicited by mass media advertising. Frequently, the desire for God gets completely lost in a constant craving for new "stuff."

Behind all our desires is our ultimate desire for union

with God and other people in love. To the extent that we become preoccupied with desires for things, to that extent we fail even to be aware of our desire for union with God. Countless people live their entire lives believing that if only they could win a lottery and become wealthy, then they would be happy. One purpose of the Tenth Commandment is to caution against such a spiritually myopic outlook on life and the world. In other words, the Tenth Commandment reminds us that the human heart can be satisfied only by loving union with God and other people.

None of the Ten Commandments has a legalistic purpose. The Decalogue is not merely a set of laws we must obey, or else. Neither is the purpose of the Commandments merely behavioral. The Ten Commandments exist to help us, with God's grace, to form in ourselves a certain kind of character, a character that lives in the world as if there is far more to reality than our senses report; as if there are invisible realities that are at least as real as what scientific observation can verify. The Tenth Commandment, in particular, helps us to live as if—contrary to the dominant Western culture—we are not what we possess. Rather, we are who and what we love.

PRAYER AND SIMPLICITY

Today, the Tenth Commandment cannot help but inspire cultural resistance, and the best defense is a strong offense. The best way to short-circuit a life of endless, exhausting, spiritually frustrating pursuit of "consumer goods" is to cultivate a life of—you guessed it—prayer. There is an infinite emptiness in the human heart that only God can fill, an endless thirst that only God can satisfy.

We're not talking about hours a day for prayer, mind you; we're simply talking about a few minutes set aside to pray in a way that works best for you. As long as you use a little time each day for prayerful openness to God's love, that can make all the difference. By doing this you remind yourself that only God can give ultimate satisfaction to the restlessness in your heart. By doing this you put some distance between yourself and a life of frantic consumption and craving to consume. Give a few minutes to prayer each day, and instead of thinking of yourself as a mere "consumer," as the dominant culture does, you will always remember that you are a child of God with a destiny far beyond and infinitely deeper than anything a consumer culture can offer.

All this is true, but at the same time we now find ourselves deep in the Tenth Commandment's implications. True as these implications are, we do not want to leave behind one aspect of the Tenth Commandment that we have yet to address. The actual wording of the Commandment is "You shall not covet *your neighbor's* goods." The main problem is with habitual "coveting" as, virtually, a way of life. But the connection to our "neighbor" is not one to overlook.

The Fourth Commandment is "You shall not steal." In the context of connections to our "neighbor," however, the Tenth Commandment carries the Fourth Commandment to a more radical level. Not only are we to not steal, but we are to not even allow ourselves to get into a situation where we might be *tempted* to steal. We are to learn to not even *think about* other people's possessions, because if we do, we might be tempted to steal.

We humans naturally desire good things that we do not have. For example, when we are hungry or thirsty we desire to eat or drink. When we are cold, we desire to be warm, and when we are hot, we desire to be cool. When we experience discomfort, we desire to be comfortable. There is nothing wrong with these desires. If we are not careful, however, our desires lead us to desire what does not belong to us or what we have no right to possess.

GREED IS NOT GOOD

From an explicitly Catholic point of view, the Tenth Commandment is about greed, the ongoing desire to accumulate material possessions endlessly. From this same perspective, the Tenth Commandment is about avarice, which is a constant craving for wealth and power. Finally, from a Catholic perspective, the Tenth Commandment is about resisting the inclination to deal with others in an unjust manner by doing harm or damage to their private possessions or property, all for the sake of my own covetous goals.

If this line of discussion begins to sound familiar, it should. To quote Menachem Kellner again:

> If we succeed in making ourselves into the kind of person who does not covet another's belongings, then the first nine of the ten commandments may be said to have done their work. We have internalized their teachings and made ourselves over. In this sense, the "tenth commandment" is not the last because it is the least important; it is the last because it leads the way through law to holiness.[3]

The *Catechism of the Catholic Church* pairs the Tenth Commandment with a saying of Jesus from the Gospel of Matthew: "For where your treasure is, there will your heart be also" (Mt 6:21).[4] For Matthew's Jesus, the issue is one of learning what to cherish and what to disregard. Of course, we need possessions, and homelessness is no ideal. But it's a question of whether we give our heart to the stuff we own, or not. Not only that, but cultural realities come into play, as well.

My wife, Kathy, and I once spent a few days in Guatemala, high in the mountains some hours' drive from Guatemala City. We visited the homes of the native people. After a day of visiting people who often live in huts constructed of dried corn stalks lashed together, with an open fire pit in the middle of a hard dirt floor, I remarked to a missionary nun about how wealthy we seem in comparison. "We have a four-bedroom house with wall-to-wall carpeting, two bathrooms, a big kitchen, many appliances, and so forth, and these people are lucky if they have one room with a wood stove and chimney in it."

The nun replied that cultures come into play, and they are real, too. So we should never feel guilty about how we live. "The important thing is that you do not forget these people and that you share what you can with them," she said.

One of the big differences between a life that observes the Tenth Commandment and one that does not is that the former actively shares. Rich, middle-class, or poor, a life that rejects covetousness is a life that shares, not just now and then but regularly. A life that observes the Tenth Commandment is a life that shares in the traditional three ways: time, talent, and treasure. For it is possible to be greedy, avaricious, and covetous with our time and talents, as well as with our financial resources.

How can we avoid becoming greedy and covetous? Sharing what we have is a prime method. The Church of Jesus Christ of Latter Day Saints (Mormons) and some evangelical Protestant religions require church members to donate a certain set percentage of their income to the church. If you don't hand over your ten percent every month, before long you're history. The Catholic Church does not take this approach, believing that giving and sharing should not be legislated. Rather, people should give from a generous heart.

Sometimes Catholicism gives human nature too much credit, however. Recent studies suggest that Catholics give far less to their parish and to various diocesan fund drives than Protestants give to their churches.

Not "coveting" has two meanings. The first is to avoid craving to own things you do not have, whether other people have them or not. The second is to share from a generous heart. As friends and followers of the risen Christ, our ideal is to care more for relationships with God and other people than we care for the constant accumulation of possessions and an ever-increasing life of affluent comfort. That's what the Tenth Commandment is about, spirit and letter.

Notes

1. Menachem Kellner, "Desire." In Rachel S. Mikva, ed., *Broken Tablets: Restoring the Ten Commandments and Ourselves* (Woodstock, VT: Jewish Lights Publishing, 1999), 129.

2. *Mishnah Torah, Laws of Robbery and Lost Property 1.10.* Quoted in Kellner, 130–131.

3. Kellner, 132.

4. See *Catechism of the Catholic Church,* n. 2534.

AFTERWORD

A businessman whose professional ethics were notorious once declared to Mark Twain, "Before I die I mean to make a pilgrimage to the Holy Land. I will climb Mount Sinai and read the Ten Commandments aloud at the top."

"I have a better idea," Twain said. "You could stay home in Boston and keep them."[1]

This witty anecdote cautions us against the general inclination to set the Ten Commandments on a pedestal, or enshrine them in a cultural vacuum. The Ten Commandments do not belong on a bronze plaque in the city square. They belong in our hearts, lived daily in the most ordinary situations, in our homes and in our workplaces. The Ten Commandments are for the real world.

Finally, there may be some residual suspicion that with the Ten Commandments God laid a heavy burden on us all, fenced us in, even condemned us to a joyless existence. On the contrary, the purpose of the Ten Commandments is not to restrict us but to liberate us from our own tendency to shoot ourselves in the foot, spiritually speaking, and in our relationships with other people. The Ten Commandments constitute "ten ways to have a full and rewarding life." They say: Life is full of good, and there are endless ways to enjoy life but only ten behaviors you need to be careful, for your own happiness, to avoid. Keep these ten "words" in mind, and you're practically home free. Ignore them, and you can

129

bet your life will go from misery to misery. Just don't say we didn't tell you.

Notes

1. Clifton Fadiman, General Ed., *The Little, Brown Book of Anecdotes* (Boston: Little, Brown & Co., 1985), 554.

ABOUT THE AUTHOR

M itch Finley is a syndicated columnist for the Catholic Sun Columns Service, and he is the author of more than twenty books, including *The Seeker's Guide to Being Catholic*; *The Joy of Being Catholic*; *Everybody Has a Guardian Angel…And Other Lasting Lessons I Learned in Catholic Schools*; *Surprising Mary*; *Meditations and Prayers on the Mother of Jesus*; *Your Family in Focus: Appreciating What You Have, Making It Even Better*; *The Joy of Being a Eucharistic Minister*; *For Men Only: Strategies for Living Catholic*; *The Catholic Virtues: Seven Pillars of a Good Life*; and, with his wife, Kathy, *Building Christian Families*. His work has appeared in dozens of religious and secular magazines and newspapers, including Reader's Digest and the Christian Science Monitor, and has received numerous awards, among which are an Excellence in Writing Award from the American Society of Journalism and Authors, the Thomas More Medal, and seven awards from the Catholic Press Association. He has a B.A. in Religious Studies from Santa Clara University and an M.A. in Theology from Marquette University. He and his wife have three sons.